The art of healthy food

Sugar Free

igloobooks

igloobooks

Published in 2017
by Igloo Books Ltd
Cottage Farm
Sywell
NN6 0BJ
www.igloobooks.com

Food photography and recipe development
© Stockfood, The Food Media Agency
Additional imagery © iStock / Getty Images
Cover image © Elena Veselova / Alamy Stock Photo

Cover designed by Nicholas Gage
Edited by Jasmin Peppiatt

HUN001 0317
2 4 6 8 10 9 7 5 3
ISBN 978-1-78670-249-4

Printed and manufactured in China

Contents

Introduction

You've probably heard a lot about sugar in the news recently. Obesity is on the rise, along with diabetes, heart disease and a host of other health problems. Many of these problems are being blamed on eating too much sugar. You may think that you keep your sugar intake under control, but many of us do not realise just how much sugar is hidden in the food we eat.

A growing problem

For thousands of years, people ate very little sugar. Honey was used sparingly as a sweetener.

However, in the last couple of centuries, as refined sugar has become cheaper and readily available, our sugar intake has massively increased. Now, many people with busy lives rely on processed food for convenience, and many of these are loaded with hidden sugar.

What to do?

If you go online, you will find a lot of conflicting advice. It can be hard to make sense of all the different opinions out there. The one thing that most experts agree on is that too much sugar is bad for you. Cutting down on the amount of sugar you eat is certainly not going to hurt you – in fact, it could help you improve your overall health.

Many people are choosing to take the plunge and cut sugar from their diet. Some try to eliminate sugar completely; others do their best to get their intake within recommended guidelines. Most people who cut down on sugar say that they feel better and look great as a result. Why not try it for yourself?

Why Cut Out Sugar?

There are a lot of compelling reasons for cutting sugar from your diet: to improve your overall health, to lose weight or even to reduce the risk of serious illnesses. Most of us eat more sugar than we should, but not everyone realises the consequences this has on our bodies.

Many foods that contain added sugar have a lot of calories with few other nutrients. Eating too much of these foods can make you overweight, which can lead to a whole host of health problems. One study found that a person's risk of dying from heart disease rose along with the percentage of sugar in their diet – no matter how young or active they were. Diabetes is the other big risk associated with eating too much sugar. Our bodies produce insulin to help break down sugar. A person with diabetes cannot produce enough insulin to cope with the sugar they eat. Left untreated, diabetes can cause complications such as stroke, nerve damage, blindness and kidney disease.

Take care of your teeth

Sugary foods and drinks are a major cause of tooth decay. Your mouth is naturally full of bacteria and when you 'feed' the bacteria with sugary foods and drinks, they break down the sugars and produce acid. This acid can decay the surface of your teeth, causing cavities. Brushing regularly will help prevent this, but it is also important to limit your sugar intake.

Do we need sugar?

Calories are a measure of the energy a food contains. Sugar provides energy that we need, but it is only one source of energy. We should aim to get most of our calories from other kinds of food, such as lean proteins, starchy foods and fresh fruits and vegetables.

Types of Sugar

When you think of sugar, you probably think of white granulated sugar, but sugar comes in many forms. Some types are found naturally in foods, while others are added during cooking or processing.

Most of the sugar that we add to our food is sucrose, which comes from either sugar cane or sugar beets. The juice is extracted from the plants and impurities are removed. Then the juice is crystallised into what we call 'refined sugar'. Whether it comes from sugar cane or sugar beets, the end product is identical. Demerara sugar and brown sugar are made using the same process. They are a bit less refined but just as full of empty calories.

Not created equally

The glycaemic index (GI) measures by how much, gram for gram, a substance raises your blood glucose level compared to glucose. Foods with a high glycaemic index, such as sucrose, are broken down quickly and release glucose rapidly into the bloodstream, giving you a 'sugar rush' that quickly fades. Foods with a low glycaemic index release glucose slowly, giving you energy over a longer period of time.

Natural sugars

Fruit contains a type of sugar called fructose. Fructose occurs naturally in the fruit and is not added. Fructose has a lower glycaemic index than sucrose, so it is safer for diabetics, but everyone should still limit the amount of fructose they eat.

Sugar substitutes

Scientists have developed a range of substances with the sweetness of sugar but fewer calories. If you love the taste of sweet things, these artificial sweeteners can deliver the taste of sugar with virtually no calories. They do not harm your teeth, and diabetics can eat them more safely than sugar. However, they are best eaten in moderation. Stevia, a sugar substitute from the stevia plant, is a natural product with many of the same benefits. Agave nectar, brown rice syrup and maple syrup are all examples of sugar substitutes that release energy more slowly than sugar.

How Much is Enough?

As scientists learn more about the effects of sugar on the body, the recommendations change. For many years the advice was to limit added sugars to ten per cent or lower of your calorie intake. This works out at about 70 grams (2 ½ oz) per day for men and 50 grams (1 ⁴/₅ oz) for women, though it varies depending on your weight and how active you are.

To put it into perspective, one teaspoon of sugar is about 4 grams (¹/₅ oz), so the average woman is recommended to have no more than 12 teaspoons of sugar a day. That may sound like a lot, but a regular-sized can of soft drink has about nine teaspoons of sugar, and some chocolate bars have in excess of eight teaspoons. Add a yogurt or a bowl of breakfast cereal and you can use up your daily allowance before you realise it.

Going lower

The World Health Organization (WHO) has recently published new recommendations calling for adults to cut their sugar intake in half – to about six teaspoons a day. To achieve this, you will have to be really smart about what you eat. Natural sugars, such as those found in fruit, are not included in the six teaspoons but many types of processed food have added sugar. For example, a tablespoon of tomato ketchup can contain a teaspoon of sugar.

Taking the right steps

To cut added sugars from your diet you will have to be disciplined. Reading food labels carefully is a huge part of this, and reducing your intake of processed foods is another key step. If you make your meals yourself from fresh ingredients, you will know exactly what goes in them.

Going Sugar-free

So you have had a look at the evidence and decided to cut sugar from your diet. Congratulations! It won't always be easy, but people all over the world are already seeing the benefits of reduced sugar intake – and now you can join them.

Keep a diary

You may think that your sugar intake is fairly low, but most of us eat more sugar than we realise. Keep a detailed food diary for a few days, recording everything you eat and drink. Check labels carefully to work out your total sugar intake. That will give you a good starting point for setting targets when you start to go sugar-free.

How low can you go?

If you search online, you will find many different approaches to going sugar-free. Many people focus on eliminating added sugar from their diet. Others take it a step further and eliminate all foods containing sugar, even natural sugars such as those found in fruit. How far you want to go is up to you. Your body doesn't need sugar, so it won't be harmed by eliminating it completely. However, fruits have a lot of other nutrients that are good for you. Most doctors recommend limiting the amount of fruit you eat, but not cutting it out entirely.

Cutting sugar out of your diet is definitely a challenge, but it does not have to be an all-or-nothing exercise. If you reduce your sugar intake slowly, while still allowing yourself a few occasional treats, you will still feel some of the health benefits. Once you start cutting out sugar, you will soon get used to it and be able to cut out even more. The lower you go, the better you will feel.

Take it slow

If you are used to having sugar in your diet, suddenly cutting it out entirely will be a shock to the system. You might manage a few days of the new regime and then give up. It is much more effective to reduce your sugar intake gradually, over a few weeks or months. This gives your body a chance to adjust to the new diet. For example, you can start to reduce the amount of sugar you put in tea or coffee, or cut down on the number of fizzy drinks you have. Once that feels 'normal', you can reduce it further.

You may feel tired at first when you start cutting out sugar. Some people experience headaches and cravings for sweet things. Make sure you are eating a healthy, balanced diet and try a piece of fruit to fend off sugar cravings. Soon your body will be used to it and you will feel great.

Feeling good

Once you are used to having less sugar, you will start to feel – and see – changes in your body. Many people who go sugar-free report that they feel less hungry and have more energy. This is because your body uses up sugar quickly but energy from other sources, such as vegetables, is much longer-lasting. You will probably also start to lose weight.

Keep it simple

At first, going sugar-free will take up time. You will be spending more time reading labels, planning meals and trying new recipes. If you try to do it at the same time as taking on a big project at work, or planning a holiday or wedding, for example, you might feel overwhelmed. Choose a time when you can focus on your diet without too many distractions. Once you are into the swing of it, things will go back to normal.

Reading Food Labels

Sometimes it is not obvious how much sugar a particular food contains. If you want to cut out sugar, you will need to read nutrition labels carefully. Have a look at the labels on the foods in your cupboards and your fridge – you will probably be amazed at how much sugar some of them have.

What to look for

Nutrition labels show the amount of sugar per 100 g (3 ½ oz) of food, which makes it easy to compare different foods. Find the figure for 'Carbohydrates (of which sugars)' on the label. If the figure is more than 22.5 g (¾ oz) of total sugars per 100 g (3 ½ oz), that is considered to be a high amount of sugar. Anything with 5 g or fewer per 100 g (3 ½ oz) is low sugar.

These figures include natural sugars, such as those found in fruit and milk, as well as added sugars. If you have two foods that have the same total amount of sugar, but one is high in milk and fruit, it is a better choice.

Traffic lights

Some foods have labels on the front of the packaging that show you at a glance whether they are high in sugar. They usually use a traffic-light system: red for high, amber for medium and green for low. If you're rushing to finish your shop and don't have time to read the ingredients lists, ditch the red foods and make sure that your basket is filled with green ones.

It doesn't take an expert to realise that foods such as sweets, biscuits, cakes and chocolate have a lot of sugar. However, many other packaged foods can have surprisingly high amounts of added sugar too. Reading labels carefully will help you cut out added sugars from your diet.

Sugar by a different name

All packaged foods are required to list their ingredients by order of weight, so the first names on the list make up the bulk of the food. Added sugars can sometimes be camouflaged when they appear in ingredients lists. Here are some other terms you might see:

sucrose • glucose • maltose • barley malt • hydrolysed starch • invert sugar • fruit juice concentrate • corn syrup •

These are all types of added sugar. If you find them near the top of the ingredients list, stay away.

What Not to Eat

Steering clear of chocolate breakfast cereals is a no-brainer, but even some of the seemingly healthier brands can have a lot of added sugar. Don't be fooled by packets that say 'reduced sugar', 'enriched' or 'wholegrain' – these labels can make a product look healthy but the nutrition label will tell you the truth. Some foods, such as yogurts, that are advertised as 'fat-free' often have a lot of sugar added to make up for the flavour lost when fat is removed.

Make your own

Have you ever made your own pasta sauce? Now is a great time to start! Jars of pasta sauce often contain a lot of added sugar, but if you make your own you will know it is sugar, free. It is easier than you might think, and you can make a big batch and freeze portions for another day.

Drinks

Fizzy drinks are one of the biggest no-nos if you want to go sugar-free. A single can of soft drink can contain more than half the recommended daily limit. Diet soft drinks are lower in sugar but have no real nutritional value. If you cannot survive without fizzy drinks, try diluting unsweetened fruit juice with sparkling water. But watch out for juice drinks that are sweetened with added sugar!

Alcoholic drinks contain sugar but some are better than others. For example, a dry red wine has less sugar than white wine. You should avoid champagne and sweet dessert wines. Spirits such as gin, vodka and whisky are low in sugar, but be careful of mixers – they are usually full of sugar. Stick to soda water, diet or slimline mixers, or drink it neat.

Low-sugar Stars

It is easy to look at a list of high-sugar foods and wonder what is left that is 'safe' to eat. Luckily, there is a huge range of low-sugar foods available. Even a picky eater will find plenty of healthy foods to choose from.

Meat and fish

Lean meats and fish are a great low-sugar option because they are packed with protein and other nutrients. Watch out for sugar-cured meats, such as some types of ham, and sauces or marinades that might be high in sugar. Eggs, beans and unsalted nuts are also good sources of low-sugar protein.

Go green

Vegetables are one of the best options
for a sugar-free diet because most
are very low in natural sugars. A few
to watch out for are beetroot, carrot
and parsnip, which contain a higher
amount of natural sugar. You can still
eat them, just in moderation. Broccoli,
asparagus, beans and sweet potatoes
are full of nutrients and low in sugar.

Grains

Carbohydrates are found in grains
such as wheat. Your body turns
carbohydrates into sugars, so many
people on a sugar-free diet try to limit
the carbohydrates they consume.
As a general rule, stay away from
refined white flour and foods made
from it, such as white bread and
pasta. Other grains, such as oats and
brown rice, are much healthier. When
choosing bread products, look out for
'wholegrain' on the label and make
sure to check for added sugar.

Breakfast

When it comes to breakfast, plain
porridge is a low-sugar winner but
if you prefer toast, you can still eat
it. Make sure to choose wholegrain
bread and replace jam or chocolate
spreads with cream cheese.

Fruit: Friend or Foe?

One of the main topics of debate among people going sugar-free is whether or not to eat fruit. Fruit contains fructose, a type of natural sugar, so many people eliminate it from their diets along with refined and added sugars. However, it is not so simple. Unlike refined sugar, fruits contain a lot of useful nutrients including fibre, vitamin C, folic acid and potassium.

Many doctors and nutritionists recommend keeping fruit in your diet but limiting the quantity you eat – two pieces a day is a common guideline. Vegetables have many of the same nutrients as fruits but fewer calories and less sugar, so replace fruits with vegetables wherever you can. When you eat fruit, make sure it is as low-sugar as possible. For example, choose tins of fruit in juice rather than in syrup.

The best fruits

In nutritional terms, no two fruits are alike. Some have more fructose and fibre than others. As a general rule, you should avoid fruits that have a high fructose content but little fibre, and try to eat those with high fibre and low fructose.

Instead of...	Eat
Grapes	Raspberries
Apple	Pear
Banana	Kiwi fruit
Cherries	Cranberries
Watermelon	Blueberries

No juice!

Sugars in fruits are less likely to cause tooth decay because of the way the sugars are contained within the structure of the fruit. When fruit is turned into juice, the sugars are released, so it's best to cut out fruit juice and stick to eating whole fruit and drinking water instead.

Eating Out

Eating a meal at a restaurant with friends is one of life's great joys, but you don't always know exactly what goes into the food. How can you stick to a sugar-free diet while eating out? It definitely takes more willpower than eating at home. Here are a few tips to help you:

- Arrive with a positive mindset – be excited about what you *can* eat rather than focusing on what you can't

- Order a starter and a main meal rather than a main meal and a dessert

- Stick to fish, meat and vegetables when choosing your food

Be prepared

If you are going to eat out, you might be able to plan ahead. Some restaurants have nutritional information for their menus posted on their websites. Have a look before you go out and choose an option that is sugar-free, or at least low in sugar.

- Go easy on condiments and salad dressings – these often have a lot of sugar. A plain vinaigrette dressing is usually low in sugar but watch out for balsamic vinegar, which is high in sugar

- Avoid dishes with tomato-based or fruity sauces

- Ask the waiter about the menu – because many people are choosing to go sugar-free, restaurants are used to being asked which dishes are lowest in sugar

- Don't be afraid to order your food exactly as you want it. If there is a sauce that might be sugary, ask to have it left off your plate

- Go for sparkling water rather than a fizzy drink. If you want alcohol, choose a small glass of dry red wine

- If your friends try to tempt you into eating a sugary treat, be firm and explain how much better you are feeling as a result of your new diet

Being Active, Staying Safe

Going sugar-free is just one part of a new, healthier lifestyle. If you seriously reduce your sugar intake, you will probably lose weight, and if you increase the amount of exercise you do then you will lose even more. Being active does not have to mean joining a gym or doing a sport you hate – even small changes in your daily routine can have a positive impact.

You don't have to break a sweat to get the benefit from exercise. It's all about keeping moving throughout the day and you can work it into things you already do. Instead of using the lift, take the stairs. Walk about while you talk on the phone. Get off the bus two or three stops earlier and walk the rest of the way. If you are driving to the shops, park a bit further away than usual. Little things like this can really add up!

If you are ready to step it up a bit, jogging, cycling and swimming are great ways to burn calories. Don't worry if you are stuck indoors – put on some music and dance around the house or give the housework some extra oomph!

Feel the benefits

Keeping active is great for your health. It helps keep your heart healthy, reduces your risk of serious illness and strengthens muscles and bones. It can make you lose weight more quickly and often leaves you feeling more energetic.

Working together

Find a friend who is also trying to be more active. If you have someone to exercise with, you'll be more motivated to keep it up. Taking a short walk at lunch with a work colleague will burn calories – and it's a great excuse for a chat, too!

Is it safe?

Going sugar-free is just like any other major lifestyle change – you should make sure you are ready for it. Even if you are in good health, it's best to talk to your doctor before you start. He or she can make sure your body can cope with a change in diet and maybe even provide some useful tips!

It is especially important to talk to your doctor if you are pregnant or trying to become pregnant, if you have a history of eating disorders or if you have any other health concerns. Your doctor might want to do a blood test for diabetes before you start, especially if you have a history of it in your family.

Ready to go

Before you start, have a look through your kitchen and get rid of anything that is going to tempt you. So often we eat things just because they are there, not because we are particularly hungry. If your cupboards are full of biscuits, it is going to be hard to stick to a sugar-free diet. Make a fresh start by filling your cupboards and fridge with healthy snacks such as nuts and carrot sticks.

Tell your friends and family about your new regime. If they know what you are doing, they can offer help and support – and they will not tempt you with offers of sweet treats. They might even want to join in! Any kind of lifestyle change is easier if you're not doing it alone.

Keep track

Before you start your sugar-free diet, step on the scales and take a photo of yourself so that you can make comparisons once you lose weight. Make a note of your measurements – sometimes it can feel like the weight loss is slow, but you'll probably be losing centimetres.

Keeping Motivated

Sticking to any kind of new routine is easiest if you have a clear idea why you are doing it. You also have to know what you want to get out of it. Sit down and make a list of your reasons for going sugar-free. If you hang it somewhere visible, then you can look at it any time you feel like you can't do it. Reminding yourself of all those health benefits can give you the motivation to keep going.

Make a plan

Think about how you want to cut down your sugar intake. If you are doing it gradually rather than cold turkey, write down a plan to show your targets, week by week. You might even choose some low-sugar recipes to try each week. It is easy to get so busy that you just want to make things easier by going back to your old routine. If you already have a plan in place, you'll be more likely to stick with it.

Setting goals

What do you hope to get out of going sugar-free? Most people want to improve their health and lose weight. Think about your short-term and long-term goals. Set yourself a realistic target weight and make a plan for how to get there.

Support from friends

Share your plans and goals with a close friend. He or she can help you keep track of your progress and offer encouragement and support – as well as a big hug when you reach your goals!

Reward yourself

Set up a star chart for yourself. It works for children, so why not for you? Every day that you stick to your sugar limits, give yourself a star. Once you have enough stars you can reward yourself with a prize, such as a magazine or a new item of clothing.

Breakfast

Breakfast

A healthy, sugar-free breakfast can provide long-lasting energy that will keep you from snacking later in the morning.

From breakfast cereal to sweetened tea, it is easy to let the sugar add up when having breakfast. Make sure to read the labels and know exactly what you are eating – for example, many breakfast cereals have a lot of added sugar. Wholegrain options, such as plain shredded wheat, are good choices. Muesli may seem like a healthy option but some shop-bought varieties are loaded with sugar. If you prefer toast, use wholegrain bread and a savoury spread such as low-fat cream cheese or avocado. A vegetable omelette is quick to prepare and full of nutrients. Scrambled eggs with smoked salmon provide protein that will keep you going until lunchtime.

If you really need a hit of sweetness to get you going in the morning, do it the healthy way, by adding a handful of fresh berries to whatever you are eating.

Green Omelette with Salmon

Serves: 4
Preparation time: 10–15 minutes
Cooking time: 6–8 minutes

Ingredients

8 large eggs, separated
110 ml / 4 fl. oz / ½ cup fat-free milk
55 g / 2 oz / ⅓ cup buckwheat flour
a large handful of cress, washed and dried
1 tbsp unsalted butter
75 g / 3 oz / ½ cup smoked salmon slices
2 tbsp low-fat plain yogurt, to serve
salt and freshly ground black pepper

Method

1. Preheat the oven to 180°C (160°C fan) / 350F / gas 4.

2. Combine 8 egg yolks and 6 whites in a food processor with the milk, flour, most of the cress and some seasoning. Blitz until smooth, then pour into a bowl.

3. Briefly whisk the remaining egg whites with a pinch of salt until softly peaked, then fold into the batter.

4. Heat the butter in a large, heatproof non-stick frying pan set over a moderate heat.

5. Add the batter and let it set for 2 minutes. Transfer the pan to the oven to finish cooking for 6–8 minutes. Remove from the oven and leave to cool slightly, then turn out and slice.

6. Serve on plates with the remaining cress, smoked salmon and a little plain yogurt.

Muesli with Raspberries

Serves: 4
Preparation time: 5 minutes
Cooking time: 5 minutes

Ingredients

300 g / 10 ½ oz / 2 cups rolled oats

55 g / 2 oz / ⅓ cup raisins

2 tbsp walnuts

75 g / 3 oz / ½ cup dried apricots, chopped

110 g / 4 oz / ⅔ cup raspberries

110 g / 4 oz / ½ cup plain yogurt

Method

1. Mix together the oats, raisins and walnuts in a large mixing bowl.

2. Divide between cereal bowls and top with the apricots, raspberries and a generous dollop of yogurt.

3. Serve immediately.

Apple and Walnut Porridge

Serves: 4
Preparation time: 5 minutes
Cooking time: 6–7 minutes

Ingredients

150 g / 5 oz / 1 ½ cups rolled oats

450 ml / 16 fl. oz / 2 cups semi-skimmed milk

375 ml / 13 fl. oz / 1 ½ cups cold water

2 small Gala or Fuji apples, cored
    and chopped

55 g / 2 oz / ½ cup walnuts, crushed

2 tsp ground cinnamon

Method

1. Combine the oats, milk and water in a large, heavy-based saucepan set over a medium heat.

2. Bring the liquid to a simmer and cook steadily for 6–7 minutes, stirring frequently, until thickened and creamy.

3. Spoon into bowls and top with chopped apple, crushed walnuts and a sprinkling of ground cinnamon before serving.

English Breakfast

Serves: 4
Preparation time: 5 minutes
Cooking time: 10–15 minutes

Ingredients

75 ml / 3 fl. oz / $\frac{1}{3}$ cup hot water

1 ½ tbsp tomato purée

1 tsp Worcestershire sauce

300 g / 10 ½ oz / 1 ½ cups canned white haricot beans, drained

4 rashers of back bacon

4 pork sausages

2 medium salad tomatoes, halved horizontally

1 tbsp unsalted butter

100 g / 3 ½ oz / 1 ½ cups button mushrooms, chopped

1 tbsp sunflower oil

4 medium eggs

4 slices of white sandwich bread

salt and freshly ground black pepper

Method

1. Preheat the grill to hot. Whisk together the hot water, tomato purée, Worcestershire sauce and seasoning in a pan. Add the beans and cook over a low heat, stirring, until soft. Season to taste.

2. Arrange the bacon, sausages and halved tomatoes on a grilling tray. Season the tomatoes. Grill the bacon and tomatoes for 2–3 minutes on both sides, then remove from the tray. Grill the sausages for a further 3–4 minutes, turning occasionally, until cooked through.

3. Meanwhile, melt the butter in a frying pan set over a moderate heat. Sauté the mushrooms for 3–4 minutes, with seasoning, until golden. Remove from the pan, wipe clean, and add the oil.

4. Fry the eggs until the white and yolks are set. Toast the slices of bread under the grill or in a toaster until golden; cut in half diagonally and serve with the rest of the cooked breakfast.

Coddled Egg
with Ham

Serves: 4
Preparation time: 5–10 minutes
Cooking time: 3–4 minutes

Ingredients

2 tbsp olive oil

4 slices of prosciutto

75 g / 3 oz / ½ cup cherry tomatoes, halved

4 large eggs

2 tbsp Parmesan, finely grated

2 tbsp balsamic vinegar

a few sprigs of thyme

salt and freshly ground black pepper

Method

1. Grease four individual ramekins with the olive oil.

2. Line with the prosciutto and cherry tomatoes, then crack in the eggs.

3. Top with Parmesan, balsamic, thyme and seasoning then sit in a large saucepan.

4. Fill the saucepan with boiling water so that it reaches halfway up the sides of the ramekins. Place the saucepan over a medium heat and cover with a lid.

5. Leave the eggs to cook for 3–4 minutes until set.

6. Once set, carefully remove from the saucepan before serving.

Green Tea Bagels

Makes: 4
Preparation time: 1 hour 5–10 minutes
Cooking time: 20 minutes

Ingredients

200 g / 7 oz / 1 ⅓ cups strong white bread
flour, plus extra for dusting

100 ml / 3 ½ fl. oz / ½ cup cold water

2 tsp matcha green tea powder

1 ½ tsp salt

¾ tsp dried fast action yeast

Method

1. Combine the flour, water, matcha powder, salt
and yeast, and mix well until a dough forms.
Turn out onto a floured surface and knead
for 10–12 minutes. Divide the dough into four
pieces and roll into balls. Cover loosely with
oiled cling film and leave to rest for 15 minutes.

2. Roll out each piece into a 15 cm x 8 cm (6 in x
3 in) oval on a floured surface, then shape into a
thick sausage, roughly 3–4 cm (1 ½ in) wide.

3. Join both ends to make rough doughnut
shapes. Seal well and leave to rest in a warm
place for 30 minutes as you preheat the oven to
180°C (160°C fan) / 350F / gas 4.

4. Bring a saucepan of water to the boil and drop
in the bagels. Cook for 30 seconds, flip and
cook the other sides for 30 seconds.

5. Remove and pat dry, then bake for 20 minutes.
Allow to cool before serving.

Blueberry Muesli

Serves: 4–6
Preparation time: 5 minutes
Cooking time: 5 minutes

Ingredients

350 g / 12 oz / 2 ⅓ cups rolled oats

75 g / 3 oz / ½ cup sultanas

2 tbsp raisins

2 tbsp golden sultanas

2 tbsp dried banana chips

450 g / 1 lb / 2 cups low-fat yogurt

100 g / 3 ½ oz / ⅔ cup blueberries

Method

1. Heat a large frying pan over a medium heat until hot.

2. Add the oats and dry fry for 30–40 seconds until they start to toast and become fragrant.

3. Pour into a large mixing bowl and add the sultanas, raisins, golden sultanas and banana chips.

4. Stir well. The muesli can now be stored in airtight container.

5. To serve, spoon some muesli into serving bowls and top with yogurt.

6. Sprinkle over a little more muesli before topping with blueberries and serving.

Coddled Egg with Salmon

Serves: 4
Preparation time: 5 minutes
Cooking time: 3–4 minutes

Ingredients

1 tbsp unsalted butter

100 g / 3 ½ oz / ⅔ cup smoked salmon
   trimmings

4 large eggs

a few sprigs of tarragon, to garnish

salt and freshly ground black pepper

Method

1. Grease four glass ramekins with
   the butter.

2. Arrange the smoked salmon trimmings
   in each ramekin, then crack one egg into
   each ramekin.

3. Season and arrange the ramekins in a large,
   heavy-based saucepan or casserole dish.

4. Pour in enough boiling water around the
   ramekins to reach halfway up them.

5. Cover the saucepan with a lid and cook
   over a low heat for 3–4 minutes until the
   eggs are set.

6. Remove from the saucepan and serve
   immediately with a sprig of tarragon on top
   as a garnish.

Soft-boiled Egg with Asparagus

Serves: 4
Preparation time: 10–15 minutes
Cooking time: 10 minutes

Ingredients

6 small eggs
50 g / 2 oz / ⅓ cup plain (all-purpose) flour
150 g / 5 oz / 1 cup panko breadcrumbs
55 ml / 2 fl. oz / ¼ cup sunflower oil
salt and freshly ground black pepper

Method

1. Bring a saucepan of salted water to the boil, and blanch the asparagus for 2 minutes.

2. Drain well and pat dry, then leave to cool.

3. Boil four of the eggs for 8 minutes. Remove and run under cold, running water for 1 minute and leave to cool to one side.

4. Season the flour and whisk the remaining eggs in a bowl with some seasoning.

5. Dust the asparagus in flour, shaking off any excess, then dip in the egg to coat. Roll in the breadcrumbs and place on a lined plate.

6. Heat the oil in a wide-rimmed frying or sauté pan until hot.

7. Shallow-fry the asparagus spears until golden and crisp on the outside. Drain, then serve alongside the soft-boiled eggs in cups.

Stack of Pancakes

Serves: 4–6
Preparation time: 5–10 minutes
Cooking time: 15 minutes

Ingredients

200 g / 7 oz / 1 ⅓ cups plain (all-purpose) flour

2 tsp baking powder

a pinch of salt

2 large eggs, beaten

3 tbsp unsalted butter, melted

250 ml / 9 fl. oz / 1 cup semi-skimmed milk

1 tbsp cumin seeds, to garnish

Method

1. Sift the flour into a large mixing bowl and stir through the baking powder and salt.

2. Combine the eggs with one tablespoon of the melted butter and the milk, then add to the dry ingredients and whisk well until you have a smooth batter.

3. Add a little of the remaining melted butter to a non-stick frying pan and cook small ladles of the batter until set and blistered on top.

4. Flip and cook the other sides for a further minute until set and golden.

5. Repeat this method, using a little melted butter each time, until you have used up the batter.

6. Stack the pancakes and garnish with cumin seeds on top before serving.

Buckwheat Crêpes

- -

Serves: 4
Preparation time: 15 minutes
Cooking time: 20 minutes

- -

Ingredients

3 tbsp unsalted butter, melted

150 g / 5 oz / 2 cups button mushrooms, finely chopped

125 g / 4 ½ oz / ¾ cup buckwheat flour

5 medium eggs

250 ml / 9 fl. oz / 1 cup water

1 tbsp sunflower oil

a small bunch of chives, snipped

salt and freshly ground black pepper

Method

1. Add a tablespoon of melted butter to a sauté pan set over a moderate heat. Add the mushrooms and sauté with seasoning for 4–5 minutes, stirring until tender. Set to one side.

2. Mix the flour and a teaspoon of salt in a bowl. Crack in one egg and whisk, gradually adding water until you have a smooth batter.

3. Heat the melted butter in a large crêpe pan. Add a ladle of batter to coat the base. Once the top starts to blister, flip the crêpe and cook for 1 minute. Repeat until you have four large crêpes, then set to one side.

4. Heat the oil in a frying pan set over a moderate heat. Fry the remaining eggs until the whites and yolks are set. Spoon the mushrooms into the centre of the crêpes and fold the edges around. Serve immediately with the fried egg, chives and seasoning.

Egg with Turkey Bacon

Serves: 4
Preparation time: 5 minutes
Cooking time: 10 minutes

Ingredients

4 medium eggs
1 tbsp white wine vinegar
1 tbsp sunflower oil
4 rashers of thick-cut turkey bacon
4 small slices of white sandwich bread
a few sprigs of chervil, to garnish
salt and freshly ground black pepper

Method

1. Bring a large saucepan of water to a simmer and stir through the white wine vinegar.

2. Crack the eggs into cups, then gently tip into the simmering water. Poach at a steady simmer for 3 minutes. Remove with a slotted spoon to kitchen paper to drain. Cover loosely with aluminium foil to keep warm.

3. Heat the oil in a large sauté pan set over a moderate heat until hot. Fry the turkey bacon for 2–3 minutes on both sides until golden brown and crisp at the edges. Drain on kitchen paper, then cut into strips.

4. Toast the slices of bread in a toaster until golden. Remove, cut off the crusts and cut into soldiers. Arrange the soldiers on plates and sit a poached egg on top.

5. Serve with the turkey bacon, a sprig of chervil and a little seasoning.

Scrambled Eggs

Serves: 4
Preparation time: 5 minutes
Cooking time: 10 minutes

Ingredients

2 tbsp unsalted butter, cubed

150 g / 5 oz / 2 cups button mushrooms, sliced

6 large eggs

75 ml / 3 fl. oz / 1/3 cup fat-free milk

a small bunch of flat-leaf parsley

salt and freshly ground black pepper

Method

1. Add a tablespoon of cubed butter to a large sauté pan set over a moderate heat until hot.

2. Add the mushrooms and a little seasoning, and sauté for 5–6 minutes, stirring and tossing occasionally, until tender.

3. Meanwhile, whisk together the eggs with the milk and the remaining butter. Pour into a heavy-based saucepan set over a medium heat.

4. Cook, stirring frequently, until the egg starts to scramble and thicken.

5. Adjust the seasoning to taste and finely chop some of the parsley.

6. Stir the chopped parsley through the eggs, then spoon it onto plates.

7. Serve with the sautéed mushrooms and the remaining parsley as a garnish.

Smoked Salmon Blinis

Serves: 4
Preparation time: 10 minutes
Cooking time: 15–20 minutes

Ingredients

50 g / 2 oz / 1/3 cup buckwheat flour

110 g / 4 oz / 2/3 cup strong white plain
(all-purpose) flour

3/4 tsp salt

1/2 tsp baking powder

1 1/2 tsp fast-action dried yeast

150 g / 5 oz / 2/3 cup crème fraiche

175 ml / 6 fl. oz / 3/4 cup semi-skimmed milk

2 medium egg yolks

2 tbsp unsalted butter

150 g / 5 oz / 1 cup smoked salmon slices

1 lemon, juiced

200 g / 7 oz / 1 cup low-fat yogurt

a small bunch of chives, finely chopped

Method

1. Prepare the blini batter by sifting together the flours, salt and baking powder.

2. Sprinkle the yeast on top, then combine the crème fraiche and milk and heat together gently. Remove from the heat and whisk in the egg yolks until smooth. Pour on top of the flour mixture and whisk, then set to one side.

3. Melt the butter in a saucepan, then brush a blini pan with a little melted butter and heat over a moderate heat. Add small ladles of the batter to the pan and cook until set and golden underneath. Flip and cook for 1 minute, then transfer to a lined plate.

4. Stack the blinis on serving plates. Dress the smoked salmon with lemon juice, then sit on top of the stacked blinis.

5. Whisk together the yogurt and chives and serve on one side.

Light Bites and Lunches

Light Bites and Lunches

At lunchtime, it's easy to grab a sandwich, or whatever else is available, but it is worth taking the time and effort to eat something healthy.

Soup is a great option for a healthy, sugar-free lunch. Bought soups often have a lot of salt and some added sugar so try making your own. You can make a big batch and freeze it in individual portions.

Salads are another perfect sugar-free choice for lunch. Just make sure you do not undo all your good work by slathering on a sugar-laden dressing. Rather, make your own by mixing olive oil and lemon juice.

The lunch ideas in this section can be eaten at other times of the day, too, and would even work as dinners. Mix and match and see which ones work best for you!

Cherry Tomato Soup

Serves: 4
Preparation time: 25 minutes
Cooking time: 50–55 minutes

Ingredients

2 tbsp olive oil

1 medium onion, finely chopped

1 medium carrot, finely chopped

1 stick of celery, finely chopped

2 tbsp tomato purée

850 g / 1 lb 14 oz / 5 ²/₃ cups mixed cherry
   tomatoes, halved

1.2 l / 2 pints / 5 cups vegetable stock, hot

175 ml / 6 fl. oz / ¾ cup passata

a few bay leaves, to garnish

flaked sea salt and freshly ground
   black pepper

Method

1. Heat the olive oil in a large saucepan over a
   medium-low heat until hot, then add the onion,
   carrot and celery.

2. Sweat for 8–10 minutes with a little salt until
   they start to brown, then stir in the tomato
   purée and three-quarters of the cherry
   tomatoes.

3. Cover the saucepan and allow the tomatoes to
   stew for 10 minutes over a low heat.

4. Remove the cover after 10 minutes and stir in
   the stock and passata. Bring to a simmer and
   cook over a reduced heat for 25–30 minutes,
   stirring occasionally.

5. Blend the soup with a stick blender until
   smooth. Return the soup to a simmer in the
   saucepan and season to taste.

6. Ladle into bowls and garnish with the
   remaining cherry tomatoes, bay leaves and
   extra seasoning.

Tuna Stew in Granary Buns

Serves: 4
Preparation time: 10 minutes
Cooking time: 15–20 minutes

Ingredients

2 tbsp olive oil

2 small courgettes (zucchinis), finely diced

2 small carrots, peeled and finely diced

a small sprig of rosemary, chopped

1 clove of garlic, minced

300 g / 10 ½ oz / 2 cups canned tuna chunks, drained

275 g / 10 oz / 1 ¾ cups passata

75 ml / 3 fl. oz / ⅓ cup cold water

4 seeded granary buns, split

salt and freshly ground black pepper

Method

1. Heat the olive oil in a casserole dish set over a medium heat until hot.

2. Add the courgette and carrot with a little seasoning. Sweat for 6–7 minutes, stirring frequently, until softened.

3. Add the rosemary and garlic and cook for 1 minute, then add the tuna, passata and water.

4. Stir well and bring the stew to a gentle simmer. Leave to cook for 8–10 minutes, stirring occasionally, until thickened.

5. Adjust the seasoning to taste and leave the stew to cool slightly before spooning into the granary buns.

6. Serve immediately.

Penne and Seafood Salad

Serves: 4
Preparation time: 20 minutes
Cooking time: 12–15 minutes

Ingredients

350 g / 12 oz / 3 cups penne pasta

150 g / 5 oz / 3 cups mixed leaf salad

2 sheets of dried wakame seaweed

2 tbsp sunflower oil

300 g / 10 ½ oz piece of salmon fillet, cubed

150 g / 5 oz / 1 cup crayfish tails

a large handful of crispy shredded seaweed

75 ml / 3 fl. oz / ⅓ cup dark soy sauce,
    to serve

a few sprigs of coriander (cilantro)

salt and freshly ground black pepper

Method

1. Preheat the grill to hot and cook the pasta in a large saucepan of salted, boiling water until 'al dente'.

2. Drain well and leave to cool to one side. Soak the sheets of wakame seaweed in a bowl of boiling water until tender, then drain and chop.

3. Coat the cubed salmon and crayfish tails in sunflower oil and season well.

4. Arrange on a grilling tray and grill for 4–5 minutes until the salmon is golden and crisp.

5. Remove from the grill and leave to cool for 5 minutes, then toss with the penne pasta, crispy seaweed and wakame seaweed.

6. Season to taste and serve in bowls with the mixed leaf salad, coriander and pots of soy sauce on the side.

Turkey, Brie and Avocado Slices

Serves: 4
Preparation time: 5 minutes
Cooking time: 5 minutes

Ingredients

100 g / 3 ½ oz piece of Brie

150 g / 5 oz / 1 cup turkey slices

4 thick slices of wholemeal baguette

1 large ripe avocado, pitted and sliced

Method

1. Cut the piece of Brie into four even slices using a warm, wet knife.

2. Fold the slices of turkey and arrange on top of the slices of baguette.

3. Top with the Brie and then avocado slices; serve immediately.

Brown Rice Veggie Burger

Makes: 4
Preparation time: 1 hour 5–15 minutes
Cooking time: 6–8 minutes

Ingredients

3 tbsp sunflower oil

1 small red onion, finely chopped

2 cloves of garlic, minced

150 g / 5 oz / 1 cup yellow split peas

100 g / 3 ½ oz / ½ cup brown rice

600 ml / 1 pint 2 fl. oz / 2 ½ cups vegetable stock

150 g / 5 oz / 1 cup dried breadcrumbs

a small bunch of flat-leaf parsley, finely chopped

3 tbsp plain yogurt

1 tbsp low-fat mayonnaise

a pinch of smoked paprika

4 seeded burger buns, split

1 small Romaine lettuce, leaves separated

salt and freshly ground black pepper

Method

1. Heat 1 tbsp of sunflower oil over a medium heat. Add the onion and garlic and sweat for 3–4 minutes, then stir in the peas and rice.

2. Stir well and cover with the stock. Bring to a simmer and cook over a low heat, covered, for 50–60 minutes until the peas and rice are tender.

3. Leave the mixture to cool slightly, then spoon into a food processor. Pulse until just combined and tip into a mixing bowl. Add 100 g of the breadcrumbs and the parsley. Mix thoroughly and season. Cover and chill for 30 minutes.

4. Shape the mixture into four thick patties, then coat in the remaining breadcrumbs. Preheat the grill to hot. Drizzle the patties with the remaining oil and grill for 3–4 minutes on both sides.

5. Whisk together the yogurt, mayonnaise, paprika and a little seasoning. Assemble the buns with lettuces, patties and some sauce, and serve with the bun lids.

Lettuce and Carrot Soup

Serves: 4
Preparation time: 10 minutes
Cooking time: 17–20 minutes

Ingredients

2 tbsp olive oil

2 sticks of celery, peeled and sliced

2 small carrots, peeled and shredded

150 g / 5 oz / 2 cups button mushrooms, sliced

1 l / 1 pint 16 fl. oz / 4 cups light vegetable stock

2 small gem lettuce, sliced

a small bunch of chives, roughly chopped

salt and pepper freshly ground black pepper

Method

1. Heat the olive oil in a large saucepan set over a medium heat until hot.

2. Add the celery and a little seasoning, then sweat for 4–5 minutes, stirring occasionally.

3. Add the carrots, mushrooms and stock. Stir well and bring to a simmer, then cook over a reduced heat for 10 minutes.

4. Stir in the lettuce and continue to cook for 3–4 minutes until wilted.

5. Add the chives and adjust the seasoning to taste before ladling into bowls and serving.

Bean and Chicken Salad

Serves: 4
Preparation time: 10 minutes
Cooking time: 8–10 minutes

Ingredients

2 tbsp sunflower oil

1 tsp dried oregano

1 tsp dried basil

4 small skinless chicken breasts, trimmed and cut into large strips

200 g / 7 oz / 1 cup canned white haricot beans, drained

200 g / 7 oz / 1 cup canned butter (lima) beans, drained

1 tbsp olive oil

1 tbsp lemon juice

100 g / 3 ½ oz / 2 cups baby spinach, washed

1 red onion, finely sliced

1 red chilli (chili), sliced

75 g / 3 oz / ½ cup mixed olives

salt and pepper

Method

1. Preheat the grill to hot.

2. Whisk together the sunflower oil with the dried herbs, then add the chicken strips and toss well to coat.

3. Season the chicken and grill for 8–10 minutes, turning once, until cooked through.

4. Remove from the grill and leave to cool to one side.

5. Toss the beans with the olive oil and lemon juice in a large mixing bowl.

6. Arrange the spinach leaves on serving plates, then top with the chicken, beans, red onion, chilli and olives.

7. Serve immediately.

Warm Duck and Veggie Salad

Serves: 4
Preparation time: 25 minutes
Cooking time: 15–20 minutes

Ingredients

4 small duck breasts (skin on)

2 small red peppers, sliced

2 small yellow peppers, sliced

1 small head of broccoli, prepared into small florets

a small bunch of tarragon, chopped

3 tbsp plain yogurt

1 tbsp walnuts, crushed

salt and freshly ground black pepper

Method

1. Lightly score the fat and skin of the ducks breasts. Season well and place skin-side down in a large, heavy-based saucepan.

2. Place the saucepan over a medium heat and let the fat from the duck breasts render down until the skin starts to turn golden.

3. Once most of the fat has rendered away, tip most of it away and flip the breasts. Cook for a further 6–8 minutes until the breasts are firm, then remove and drain. Cover loosely with foil and leave to rest for 10 minutes.

4. Add the peppers and broccoli to the pan and cook them in the remaining duck fat, over a medium heat and covered, for 3–4 minutes.

5. Slice the breasts and add them to the pan, then cook for 2–3 minutes. Add the yogurt and tarragon. Stir well and cook for 1 minute, then season. Serve with crushed walnuts.

Mushroom and Yogurt

Serves: 4
Preparation time: 10 minutes

Ingredients

300 g / 10 ½ oz / 4 cups button mushrooms

200 g / 7 oz / 1 cup low-fat plain yogurt

2 tbsp reduced-fat crème fraiche

1 tbsp lemon juice

a small bunch of chives, finely chopped

salt and freshly ground black pepper

Method

1. Wash and dry the mushrooms thoroughly, then slice.

2. Whisk together the yogurt, crème fraiche, lemon juice and seasoning in a small mixing bowl until smooth.

3. Arrange the sliced mushrooms in serving cups and spoon over the yogurt sauce.

4. Garnish with chopped chives and a little more black pepper before serving.

Lettuce and Turkey Salad

Serves: 4
Preparation time: 15–20 minutes
Cooking time: 15 minutes

Ingredients

75 g / 3 oz / ⅓ cup low-fat plain yogurt

1 tbsp low-fat mayonnaise

1 tbsp lemon juice

1 tsp Worcestershire sauce

½ tsp paprika

4 small eggs

2 x 150 g / 5 oz turkey breast escalopes

1 tbsp sunflower oil

1 large round lettuce, leaves separated

2 spring onions (scallions), finely sliced

1 green chilli (chili), finely sliced

1 red chilli (chili), finely sliced

salt and freshly ground black pepper

Method

1. Whisk together the yogurt, mayonnaise, lemon juice, Worcestershire sauce, paprika and seasoning until smooth. Cover and chill.

2. Cook the eggs in a saucepan of boiling water for 12 minutes, then drain and refresh immediately in iced water.

3. Heat the sunflower oil in a large sauté set over a moderate heat until hot.

4. Season the escalopes, then pan-fry for 3–4 minutes on both sides until golden-brown.

5. Remove from the pan and leave to rest for 1 minute, then slice into thin strips.

6. Roughly tear the lettuce and arrange in serving bowls. Peel and quarter the eggs, then arrange on top of the lettuce with the turkey, spring onion and chillies. Drizzle the prepared dressing over the salads and serve.

Tapenade on Toast

Serves: 8 as an appetiser
Preparation time: 10 minutes

Ingredients

150 g / 5 oz / 1 cup sun-dried tomatoes in oil

55 g / 2 oz / $\frac{1}{3}$ cup pitted black olives

2 cloves of garlic, chopped

2 tbsp preserved anchovy fillets, drained

2 tbsp passata

a small handful of basil leaves, finely chopped

1 tbsp lemon juice

1 white baguette, cut into thin slices

salt and freshly ground black pepper

Method

1. Combine the sun-dried tomatoes, black olives, garlic, anchovy fillets, passata and a little seasoning in a food processor.

2. Blitz until a thick tapenade comes together.

3. Scrape into a mixing bowl and stir through the chopped basil and lemon juice. Season to taste.

4. Toast the slices of bread under a hot grill until golden brown on both sides.

5. Remove from the grill and leave to cool, then top with the tapenade and serve.

Pea, Watercress and Carrot Salad

Serves: 4
Preparation time: 10 minutes
Cooking time: 1 minute

Ingredients

1 mango, stoned and flesh chopped

75 ml / 3 fl. oz / ⅓ cup sunflower oil

2 tbsp white wine vinegar

150 g / 5 oz / 1 ½ cups frozen petit pois, thawed

2 large carrots, peeled

100 g / 3 ½ oz / 2 cups watercress

a few sprigs of mint, leaves picked

salt and freshly ground black pepper

Method

1. Blitz together the mango flesh, sunflower oil, white wine vinegar and seasoning in a food processor until smooth. Pour into a jug and chill until needed.

2. Blanch the petit pois in a saucepan of salted, boiling water for 1 minute, then drain and refresh in iced water.

3. Peel ribbons of carrot using a vegetable peeler, then toss with the watercress, petit pois and mint leaves in a large mixing bowl.

4. Divide between serving plates and drizzle with the mango vinaigrette before serving.

Thai Prawn Salad

Serves: 4
Preparation time: 10 minutes
Cooking time: 2–3 minutes

Ingredients

1 large clove of garlic, minced

2 tbsp fish sauce

2 tbsp rice wine vinegar

1 lime, juiced

2 tbsp light soy sauce

2 tbsp sunflower oil

350 g / 12 oz / 2 ⅓ cups peeled prawns
(shrimp), deveined

1 red chilli (chili), finely sliced

1 round lettuce, shredded

½ small cucumber, julienned

½ small onion, finely sliced

Method

1. Whisk together the garlic, fish sauce, vinegar, lime juice and soy sauce in a small bowl, then set to one side.

2. Heat the sunflower oil in a large sauté pan or wok set over a moderate heat until hot.

3. Add the prawns and chilli. Stir-fry for 2–3 minutes until the prawns are pink and tender.

4. Remove from the heat and add two tablespoons of the dressing.

5. Toss the lettuce, cucumber and onion with the remaining dressing and arrange in bowls.

6. Top with the prawns and serve immediately.

Tomato and Pepper Salad

Serves: 4
Preparation time: 5 minutes
Cooking time: 5 minutes

Ingredients

2 medium yellow peppers, diced

2 medium green peppers, diced

4 large vine tomatoes, cored and sliced into wedges

1 red onion, roughly chopped

1 small lettuce, roughly chopped

55 ml / 2 fl. oz / ¼ cup olive oil

1 tbsp white wine vinegar

1 tsp Dijon mustard

4 small white tortillas, to serve

1 tbsp Parmesan, finely grated

flaked sea salt and pepper

Method

1. Toss together the peppers, tomato wedges, lettuce and red onion with a little seasoning in a large mixing bowl.

2. Whisk together the olive oil, vinegar, Dijon mustard and seasoning in a small mixing bowl until smooth.

3. Toss the dressing with the salad to coat evenly.

4. Serve with a sprinkling of Parmesan and flaked sea salt.

Pea and Bacon Soup

Serves: 4
Preparation time: 10 minutes
Cooking time: 1 hour

Ingredients

2 tbsp olive oil

2 tbsp butter

1 onion, finely chopped

2 cloves of garlic, crushed

100 g / 3 ½ oz / ½ cup dried green split peas

1 litre / 1 pint 15 fl. oz / 4 cups fresh
    vegetable stock

300 g / 10 ½ oz / 2 cups garden peas,
    defrosted if frozen

1 tbsp flat leaf parsley, chopped

6 rashers dry-cure streaky bacon, chopped

2 tbsp Greek yogurt

Method

1. Heat the oil and butter in a saucepan and fry
   the onion for 5 minutes or until softened.

2. Add the garlic and split peas to the pan and
   cook for 2 more minutes, then stir in the
   vegetable stock.

3. Simmer for 45 minutes or until the split peas
   are starting to break down, then add the
   garden peas and parsley.

4. Blend the the soup until smooth with an
   emersion blender or in a liquidiser then
   taste and adjust the seasoning with salt
   and pepper.

5. Dry fry the bacon in a hot pan until
   golden and crisp, then stir two thirds of it
   into the soup.

6. Ladle into four warm bowls and garnish with
   Greek yogurt and the rest of the bacon.

Main Meals

Main Meals

You've stuck to your sugar-free diet for breakfast and lunch, and now it is time for a delicious dinner – you deserve it! The recipes in this section will give you loads of ideas for nutritious, sugar-free meals.

Fish is a fantastic choice: it is sugar-free, high in protein and other nutrients, and many types are low-calorie. It can be cooked in many different ways, and is usually quick to prepare, making it perfect for busy days.

Meat fits into a sugar-free diet, too. Stick to lean cuts and remove all visible fat and skin. Like other high-protein foods, meat can help you feel fuller for longer, and it also supplies vital minerals, such as iron.

Any meat or fish on your plate should be accompanied by fresh vegetables. You will quickly get tired of steamed broccoli at every meal, so now is a great time to experiment with vegetables you have never tried before. You may find something new that you absolutely love!

Swordfish with Spring Onions

Serves: 4
Preparation time: 5 minutes
Cooking time: 6–8 minutes

Ingredients

4 x 175 g / 6 oz swordfish fillets

2 tbsp sunflower oil

a few sprigs of dill, to garnish

100 g / 3 ½ oz / ²/₃ cup pitted black olives, chopped

4 spring onions (scallions), finely sliced

salt and freshly ground black pepper

Method

1. Preheat the grill to hot.

2. Brush the swordfish with oil and season generously on both sides.

3. Arrange on a grilling tray and grill for 6–8 minutes, turning once, until the flesh is firm yet slightly springy to the touch.

4. Finely chop some of the dill and sprinkle on top of the swordfish.

5. Transfer to plates and top with chopped olives and sliced spring onion. Garnish with more dill before serving.

Summer Veggie Stir-fry

Serves: 4
Preparation time: 5 minutes
Cooking time: 7 minutes

Ingredients

2 tbsp sunflower oil

2 medium yellow courgettes (zucchinis), roughly chopped

150 g / 5 oz / 1 ½ cups green (string) beans, trimmed

150 g / 5 oz / 1 ½ cups asparagus spears, trimmed with woody ends removed

4 thin spring onions (scallions)

150 g / 5 oz / 1 cup broad (fava) beans, shelled

150 g / 5 oz / 1 cup cherry tomatoes, halved

a small bunch of basil, leaves picked

salt and freshly ground black pepper

Method

1. Blanch the courgette in a saucepan of salted, boiling water for 2 minutes. Remove with a slotted spoon, then add the green beans and asparagus spears.

2. Blanch for 1 minute, then drain and pat dry. Heat a tablespoon of oil in a large wok set over a moderate heat until hot.

3. Add the courgette and stir-fry for 2 minutes, then add the beans, asparagus spears and spring onions.

4. Stir-fry for a further minute with a little seasoning, then add the remaining oil as well as the broad beans and cherry tomato halves.

5. Continue to stir-fry for another minute and adjust the seasoning to taste. Serve in a large bowl, garnished with basil leaves on top.

Stuffed Round Courgettes

Serves: 4
Preparation time: 15 minutes
Cooking time: 30–35 minutes

Ingredients

4 medium round courgettes (zucchinis)

100 g / 3 ½ oz / 1 ⅓ cups fresh breadcrumbs

75 g / 3 oz / ¾ cup mozzarella, grated

50 g / 2 oz / ⅓ cup sun-dried tomatoes, chopped

2 tbsp olive oil

salt and freshly ground black pepper

Method

1. Preheat the oven to 180°C (160°C fan) / 350F / gas 4.

2. Score light patterns in the skin of the courgettes using the edge of a peeler, then remove the tops and reserve.

3. Scoop out most of the flesh and seeds, discarding them.

4. Mix together the breadcrumbs, mozzarella, sun-dried tomato and seasoning, then spoon into the cavities.

5. Replace the tops on top of the stuffing and arrange the courgettes on a baking tray.

6. Drizzle with olive oil and bake for 30–35 minutes until the flesh is tender and the filling is piping hot.

7. Remove from the oven and leave to cool slightly before serving.

Veggie
Sausage Pasta

Serves: 4
Preparation time: 15–20 minutes
Cooking time: 15–20 minutes

Ingredients

350 g / 12 oz / 3 cups penne pasta

1 ½ tbsp sunflower oil

1 medium onion, finely chopped

1 clove of garlic, minced

75 g / 3 oz / 1 cup button mushrooms,
   finely chopped

400 g / 14 oz / 2 cups canned chopped tomatoes

4 vegetarian sausages

a few sprigs of parsley, chopped

salt and freshly ground black pepper

Method

1. Cook the pasta in a large saucepan of salted,
   boiling water until 'al dente'.

2. Meanwhile, heat the oil in a large saucepan set
   over a moderate heat until hot. Sauté the onion
   and garlic with a pinch of salt for 5–6 minutes,
   stirring frequently, until softened.

3. Add the mushrooms and continue to cook for
   3–4 minutes, then add the chopped tomatoes.

4. Stir well and bring the sauce to a simmer, then
   reduce to a low heat and cook for 8–10 minutes
   until thickened.

5. Drain the pasta well and cover loosely.

6. Heat the grill to hot and grill the sausages for
   6–7 minutes, turning occasionally. Remove from
   the grill, slice, and stir in to the sauce.

7. Adjust the seasoning to taste, then stir into the
   pasta and serve with chopped parsley on top.

Halibut with Concasse

Serves: 4
Preparation time: 10 minutes
Cooking time: 10–12 minutes

Ingredients

450 g / 1 lb piece of halibut, skinned and pin-boned

350 g / 12 oz / 2 ½ cups vine tomatoes, cored and finely chopped

75 g / 3 oz / ½ cup pitted black olives, chopped

2 tbsp sunflower oil

a small bunch of basil, leaves picked

salt and freshly ground black pepper

Method

1. Preheat the oven to 200°C (180°C fan) / 400F / gas 6.

2. Use a sharp knife to cut the halibut into four, even fillets.

3. Sit the fillets in a cast-iron or heavy-based sauté pan, then season generously.

4. Roughly mash the chopped tomatoes in a mixing bowl, then spoon on top of the fillets and top with the olives.

5. Drizzle the oil over everything and roast in the oven for 10–12 minutes; the fish will be firm yet very slightly springy to the touch when it is ready.

6. Remove the pan from the oven and garnish with the basil leaves before serving.

Salmon Satay Brochettes

Serves: 4
Preparation time: 15 minutes
Cooking time: 6–8 minutes

Ingredients

150 g / 5 oz / 1 ½ cups roasted peanuts

½ tsp salt

1 tbsp groundnut oil

55 ml / 2 fl. oz / ¼ cup warm water

1 tbsp light soy sauce

1 tbsp lime juice

450 g / 14 oz / 3 cups skinless salmon fillet, diced

350 g / 12 oz / 2 cups cooked long-grain rice

8 wooden skewers, soaked in cold water for 30 minutes beforehand

2 spring onions (scallions), finely sliced

Method

1. Blitz together the peanuts and salt in a food processor for 30–45 seconds. Scrape down the sides and continue to blitz, adding the oil slowly, until you have a smooth peanut butter.

2. Whisk together the peanut butter, water, soy sauce and lime juice in a saucepan until smooth.

3. Cook over a medium-low heat for 2–3 minutes, stirring, until simmering. Remove from the heat and cool for 5 minutes. Preheat the grill to hot.

4. Thread the salmon onto the skewers and brush with a little of the satay sauce.

5. Arrange the salmon skewers on a grilling tray. Grill for 4–5 minutes, turning once, until the flesh is firm yet slightly springy to the touch.

6. Reheat the rice, then spoon into bowls.

7. Sit the brochettes on top, brush with satay sauce and serve garnished with spring onion.

Asian-style Pork Burger

Serves: 4
Preparation time: 30–35 minutes
Cooking time: 8–10 minutes

Ingredients

175 g / 6 oz / 2 cups red jalapeno or chilli (chili) peppers, deseeded and chopped

2 cloves of garlic, minced

75 ml / 3 fl. oz / $\frac{1}{3}$ cup distilled white vinegar

2 tbsp tomato paste

1 tbsp fish sauce

150 g / 3 oz / $\frac{2}{3}$ cup low-fat yogurt

½ tsp garlic powder

a small bunch of dill, finely chopped

4 crusty white rolls, split

4 x 175 g / 6 oz pork loin steaks

1 tbsp sunflower oil

1 lime, juiced

1 tbsp fish sauce

½ white cabbage, shredded

a few large sprigs of coriander (cilantro), to garnish

salt and freshly ground black pepper

Method

1. Combine the chillies, garlic, vinegar, tomato paste, fish sauce and 1 tsp of salt in a food processor, and blitz until smooth. Pour into a pan and bring to the boil over a moderate heat. Reduce the heat and simmer for 5–10 minutes. Season and set to one side.

2. Whisk together the yogurt, garlic powder and dill with seasoning. Cover and chill. Flatten the steaks and slice each in half.

3. Whisk together the chilli sauce, oil, lime juice and fish sauce with a little pepper. Add the pork pieces and rub the marinade into them, then cover and leave for 15 minutes.

4. Preheat a grill until hot. Remove the pork shake off any excess marinade. Cook under the grill for 8–10 minutes, turning once.

5. Spread yogurt sauce onto the bun bases, top with cabbage and pieces of pork, and serve garnished with coriander and the bun lids.

Grilled Salmon with Lettuce

Serves: 4
Preparation time: 10 minutes
Cooking time: 8–10 minutes

Ingredients

75 g / 3 oz / ⅓ cup low-fat yogurt
2 tbsp cold water
2 tbsp white wine vinegar
1 tbsp Dijon mustard
1 tbsp olive oil
4 x 150 g / 5 oz pieces of salmon
2 tbsp harissa paste
2 little gem lettuces, quartered
2 large cloves of garlic, thinly sliced
½ red onion, finely sliced
1 lemon, zest pared and thinly sliced
2 tbsp sunflower oil
salt and freshly ground black pepper

Method

1. Preheat the grill to a moderately hot temperature. Whisk together the yogurt, water, vinegar, mustard and olive oil with a little seasoning until smooth and pour into a jug, chilling until needed.

2. Rub the tops of the salmon with harissa and arrange on a large grilling tray.

3. Sit the quartered lettuce next to the salmon and top with garlic, onion and lemon zest.

4. Drizzle the lettuce and salmon with sunflower oil and seasoning and grill for 6–8 minutes. Remove the lettuce after 5 minutes (the salmon will need a few extra minutes).

5. Once the salmon is firm with a spring to the touch, remove from the grill and place on plates next to the lettuce halves. Spoon a little of the prepared dressing around the plate and serve.

Asparagus and Prosciutto Salad

Serves: 4
Preparation time: 5–10 minutes
Cooking time: 10–13 minutes

Ingredients

4 medium eggs

8 thick spears of white asparagus, woody ends removed

150 g / 5 oz / 1 cup prosciutto slices

55 g / 2 oz / 1 cup watercress, washed and dried

400 g / 14 oz / 2 cups canned artichoke hearts, drained and roughly chopped

2 tbsp olive oil

salt and freshly ground black pepper

Method

1. Cook the eggs in a large saucepan of boiling water for 8–10 minutes. Drain and refresh immediately in iced water.

2. Peel the asparagus spears to remove the outer layer, then blanch in a saucepan of salted, boiling water for 2–3 minutes.

3. Drain well and leave to cool.

4. Roughly tear the slices of prosciutto and arrange on plates along with the watercress and artichoke.

5. Carefully crack and peel the eggs, then cut in half and sit next to the salad.

6. Drizzle the salad with olive oil and finish with a little salt and freshly ground black pepper before serving.

Chicken with Vegetables

Serves: 6
Preparation time: 25 minutes
Cooking time: 1 hour 30–40 minutes

Ingredients

1.5 kg / 3 lb 5 oz chicken, cleaned and trussed

2 tbsp sunflower oil

5 small carrots

3 medium purple carrots

3 medium parsnips

2 small lemons, halved

a small bunch of flat-leaf parsley, chopped

salt and freshly ground black pepper

Method

1. Preheat the oven to 180°C (160°C fan) / 350F / gas 4 and rub the chicken with a tablespoon of oil. Season generously.

2. Arrange the carrots and parsnips in the base of a roasting tin and drizzle with the remaining oil.

3. Season generously, then tuck the lemon halves between the vegetables.

4. Sit the chicken on top and place the roasting tin in the oven for 1 hour 30–40 minutes until the chicken is cooked through; the juices should run clear when the thickest part of the thigh is pierced.

5. Remove from the oven and cover loosely with aluminium foil. Leave to rest for at least 15 minutes.

6. Sprinkle the vegetables with chopped parsley before serving.

Marinated Vegetable Pizza

Serves: 4
Preparation time: 40 minutes
Cooking time: 12–15 minutes

Ingredients

1 medium aubergine (eggplant), deseeded and cut into thin strips

1 large red pepper, sliced

1 medium onion, roughly sliced

2 tbsp olive oil

150 g / 5 oz ready-made pizza dough

55 g / 2 oz / ½ cup Manchego, grated

55 g / 2 oz / ½ cup mozzarella, grated

2 tbsp preserved anchovy fillets, drained and roughly chopped

a small bunch of chives, finely chopped

a little plain (all-purpose) flour, for dusting

Method

1. Combine the aubergine, peppers and onion in a mixing bowl with the oil and a little seasoning. Stir well and leave at room temperature for up to 30 minutes.

2. Preheat the oven to 220°C (200°C fan) / 425F / gas 7 and line a large, square baking tray. Roll out the dough on a floured surface into a square approximately 25 cm x 25 cm x ½ cm (10 in x 10 in x ¼ in).

3. Carefully lift onto the prepared baking tray and top with the grated cheeses and anchovy, then top with the marinated vegetables and oil.

4. Bake for 12–15 minutes until the dough is cooked and golden brown at the edges. Remove to a wire rack to briefly cool, then sprinkle with chopped chives and serve.

Turkey Burger

Makes: 4
Preparation time: 15 minutes
Cooking time: 18–22 minutes

Ingredients

100 g / 3 ½ oz / ½ cup tomato purée

1 tbsp apple cider vinegar

a pinch of allspice

a pinch of Cayenne

½ tsp garlic powder

½ tsp onion powder

75 ml / 3 fl. oz / $^1/_3$ cup cold water

4 sesame seed burger buns, split

450 g / 1 lb / 3 cups lean turkey mince

75 g / 3 ½ oz / 1 cup fresh white
    breadcrumbs

1 tbsp sunflower oil

2 large vine tomatoes, cored and chopped

½ red onion, finely chopped

1 small shallot, finely chopped

a small bunch of basil, roughly chopped

salt and freshly ground
    black pepper

Method

1. Preheat the oven to 190°C (170°C fan) / 375F / gas
   5. Whisk together the tomato purée, vinegar, allspice,
   Cayenne, garlic powder, onion powder and water.
   Season to taste, then cover and chill.

2. Scrunch together the turkey mince and breadcrumbs
   with seasoning in a mixing bowl. Divide the mixture
   into four, the pack down and shape into patties.
   Arrange on a baking tray and drizzle with the oil.

3. Bake for 18–22 minutes until golden on the outside
   and cooked through on the inside.

4. Meanwhile, stir together the tomato, red onion,
   shallot and basil with a little seasoning in a mixing
   bowl. Cover and chill until ready to serve.

5. Spread the bun bases with the prepared ketchup,
   then sit the patties on top and spoon over some
   salsa. Serve with the bun lids.

Grilled Salmon with Vegetables

Serves: 4
Preparation time: 15 minutes
Cooking time: 18–20 minutes

Ingredients

1 tbsp olive oil

250 g / 9 oz / 1 ²/₃ cups baby turnips, trimmed

150 g / 5 oz / 1 cup baby carrots, trimmed

450 ml / 16 fl. oz / 2 cups vegetable stock

150 g / 5 oz / 1 cup asparagus spears, trimmed with woody ends removed

4 small gem lettuce, split in half

75 g / 3 oz / 1 cup chestnut mushrooms, halved

4 x 150 g / 5 oz pieces of salmon

2 small cooked beets, halved

salt and freshly ground black pepper

Method

1. Heat the olive oil in a large saucepan set over a moderate heat until hot. Add the turnips and carrots and sauté with seasoning for 2 minutes

2. Cover with the stock and simmer for 7–8 minutes, then add the asparagus and lettuce.

3. Continue to simmer for 2 minutes, then stir in the mushrooms and remove from the heat. Set to one side.

4. Preheat the grill to hot and season the salmon well before arranging, skin-side up, on a grilling tray. Grill for 7–9 minutes until the skin is crisp and the flesh is turning opaque.

5. To serve, remove the vegetables from the cooking liquor with a pair of tongs and arrange in the centre of plates.

6. Sit the salmon on top and garnish with a halved beet before serving.

Chilli con Carne with Rice

Serves: 4
Preparation time: 15–20 minutes
Cooking time: 40–50 minutes

Ingredients

1 ½ tbsp sunflower oil

1 large onion, finely chopped

2 cloves of garlic, minced

2 tsp ground cumin

1 tsp ground coriander (cilantro)

1 tsp chilli (chili) powder

½ tsp dried oregano

450 g / 1 lb / 3 cups extra lean steak mince

400 g / 14 oz / 2 cups canned chopped tomatoes

200 g / 7 oz / 1 cup canned kidney beans, drained

350 g / 12 oz / 2 cups cooked basmati rice

55 g / 2 oz / ¼ cup low-fat plain yogurt

salt and freshly ground black pepper

Method

1. Heat the oil in a large, heavy-based saucepan set over a medium heat until hot. Add the onion and garlic and sweat for 6–7 minutes, stirring occasionally.

2. Add the ground spices and herbs and stir well. Cook for 30 seconds, then add the mince. Increase the heat and cook until browned, breaking it up with a wooden spoon.

3. Stir in the chopped tomatoes and kidney beans until incorporated, then cover with a lid and simmer over a reduced heat for 30–40 minutes; stir to prevent sticking.

4. Season to taste and leave to cool for a few minutes as you reheat the rice in a microwave until piping hot.

5. Spoon the rice into bowls and top with the chilli. Garnish with a dollop of yogurt and a little seasoning on top before serving.

Squid and Veggie Wok-fry

Serves: 4
Preparation time: 5 minutes
Cooking time: 5 minutes

Ingredients

2 tbsp groundnut oil

350 g / 12 oz / 2 ⅓ cups squid tentacles, cut into rings

1 small head of broccoli, prepared into small florets

2 medium carrots, peeled and cut into thin batons

1 small green pepper, roughly sliced

1 small red pepper, roughly sliced

110 g / 4 oz / 1 ½ cups beansprouts

½ tsp dried chilli (chili) flakes

1 tbsp white sesame seeds

2 tbsp dark soy sauce

1 tbsp rice wine vinegar

Method

1. Heat a tablespoon of oil in a large wok set over a high heat until hot.

2. Add the squid rings and stir-fry for 1 minute, then remove from the wok to a plate.

3. Add the remaining tablespoon of oil, then add the broccoli and carrots. Stir-fry for 2 minutes, then add the peppers and beansprouts.

4. Return the squid rings to the wok and continue to stir-fry for 1–2 minutes. Stir in the chilli flakes, sesame seeds, soy sauce and rice wine vinegar.

5. Spoon into bowls and serve immediately.

Beef and Veggie Stir-fry

Serves: 4
Preparation time: 5–10 minutes
Cooking time: 7 minutes

Ingredients

2 tbsp groundnut oil

450 g / 1 lb skirt steak, trimmed and sliced

1 large head of broccoli, prepared into bite-sized florets

2 small red peppers, finely sliced

2 spring onions (scallions), sliced diagonally

2 tbsp light soy sauce

1 tbsp rice wine vinegar

1 tbsp white sesame seeds

1 orange, zest julienned

350 g / 12 oz / 2 cups cooked short-grain rice

salt and freshly ground black pepper

Method

1. Heat a tablespoon of the groundnut oil in a large wok set over a high temperature until hot.

2. Season the steak with salt and pepper, then stir-fry in the oil for 2 minutes. Remove from the wok.

3. Add the remaining tablespoon of oil and stir-fry the broccoli for 2 minutes, then add the peppers and spring onions and cook for a further minute.

4. Return the steak to the pan and cook over a reduced heat for a further 2 minutes. Season to taste with soy sauce and rice wine vinegar.

5. Stir through the sesame seeds and julienned orange zest at this point.

6. Reheat the rice, if necessary, and serve alongside the stir-fry.

Beef and Pepper Hash

Serves: 4
Preparation time: 5 minutes
Cooking time: 30 minutes

Ingredients

3 tbsp olive oil

225 g / 8 oz / 1 ½ cups minced beef

1 clove of garlic, crushed

½ tsp smoked Paprika, plus extra for sprinkling

½ tsp ground cumin

1 onion, finely chopped

½ red pepper, diced

½ green pepper, diced

½ yellow pepper, diced

4 leftover boiled potatoes, cooled and diced

4 large eggs

Method

1. Preheat the oven to 200°C (180°C fan) / 400F / gas 6.

2. Heat 1 tbsp of oil in a large oven-proof frying pan and fry the mince until lightly browned. Stir in the garlic, Paprika and cumin and sauté for 2 minutes, then scrape the mixture into a bowl and set aside.

3. Heat the rest of the oil in the pan and fry the onion and peppers for 10 minutes, or until soft and sweet. Add the potatoes and sauté for 5 minutes or until piping hot, then return the beef to the pan and season to taste with salt and pepper.

4. Make four hollows in the mixture and break in the eggs. Transfer the pan to the oven and bake for 5 minutes or until the egg whites have set.

5. Sprinkle the top with a little more smoked Paprika, then serve immediately.

Desserts

Desserts

Going sugar-free doesn't have to mean giving up dessert. If you are reducing rather than eliminating your sugar intake, then dessert can be the time to reward yourself with a small, sweet treat. Even if you are cutting out sugar entirely, there's still room for the occasional pudding. You'll probably find that as your body gets used to a sugar-free diet, you stop craving sweet treats after meals.

Why not choose a coffee? It makes a great way to finish off a meal. If you want something sweet, fresh fruit is a good option.

You'll probably be surprised at the number of sweet desserts that can be made without sugar. Some use sugar substitutes but others use the natural sweetness of ingredients such as fruit. Do a bit of experimenting and you will find something you love.

Lemon Yogurt Ice Cream

Makes: 1 pint
Preparation time:
3 hours 25–30 minutes

Ingredients

500 g / 1 lb 2 oz / 2 cups low-fat
   lemon yogurt

75 ml / 3 fl. oz / 1/3 cup semi-skimmed milk

2 tsp lemon extract

1 lemon, zested

Method

1. Combine the yogurt, milk and lemon extract in a food processor. Blitz until smooth.

2. Pour the liquid into an ice cream machine and churn for 15–20 minutes until frozen and creamy.

3. Scrape the frozen yogurt into a freezer-proof container and freeze until set.

4. Before serving the frozen yogurt, remove from the freezer and leave to stand for 5 minutes, the scoop out and serve with lemon zest sprinkled on top.

Summer Fruit Jelly

Serves: 4
Preparation time:
4 hours 10 minutes

Ingredients

225 g / 8 oz / 1 ½ cups strawberries,
   hulled and chopped
150 g / 5 oz / 1 cup raspberries
110 g / 4 oz / ¾ cup blackberries
75 g / 3 oz / ¾ cup redcurrants
2 tbsp sugar-free raspberry jelly powder
250 ml / 9 fl. oz / 1 cup boiling water
325 ml / 11 fl. oz / 1 ⅓ cups cold water
75 g / 3 oz / 1/3 cup low-fat plain yogurt

Method

1. Grease and line four individual ramekins
   with a sheet of cling film; make sure that
   the cling film overhangs the rims.

2. Fill the ramekins with a selection of the fruits,
   leaving a little fruit for a garnish.

3. Half fill a mixing jug with boiling water and
   sprinkle over the jelly powder. Leave to
   dissolve for a few minutes, whisk, and then
   mix in the cold water.

4. Divide the liquid between the ramekins and
   transfer to the fridge to set for at least 4
   hours or overnight.

5. Once set, carefully lift the jellies out of the
   ramekins and peel away the cling film.

6. Garnish with the reserved fruit and a dollop
   of yogurt on the side.

Fruit Gazpacho

Serves: 4–6
Preparation time: 5 minutes

Ingredients

3 large ripe bananas

200 g / 7 oz / 1 cup canned pineapple chunks in juice

375 ml / 13 fl. oz / 1 ½ cups pineapple juice

55 ml / 2 fl. oz / ¼ cup white rum (optional)

Method

1. Roughly chop the bananas and combine with three-quarters of the pineapple chunks (and their juice) as well as the pineapple juice and rum, if using.

2. Blitz until the mixture is creamy and pourable.

3. Pour into a serving jug and serve immediately with the remaining pineapple chunks on top.

Almond Jelly

Makes: 4
Preparation time: 6 hours 10 minutes
Cooking time: 10 minutes

Ingredients

600 ml / 1 pint 2 fl. oz / 3 cups plain
   almond milk

4 tsp gelatin powder

½ tsp vanilla extract

½ tsp almond extract

2 tbsp almonds, to garnish

Method

1. Grease the insides of four individual ramekins
   with non-stick cooking spray. Mix the gelatin
   with two tablespoons of cold water in a small
   bowl and leave for 2 minutes.

2. Combine the almond milk, vanilla and almond
   extract in a saucepan, then bring to a simmer
   over a medium heat.

3. Remove from the heat and pour a little into
   the gelatin mixture. Whisk and leave for 1
   minute, then whisk back into the almond milk
   in the saucepan. Let the liquid cool slightly,
   then divide between the ramekins and cover
   and chill for at least 6 hours until set.

4. Once set, dip the ramekins into a bowl of
   boiling water and carefully tip out onto plates.

5. Crush some of the almonds and spoon on
   top as a garnish, serving the rest on the side.

Fraisier-style Verrine

Serves: 4
Preparation time: 15 minutes
Cooking time: 5 minutes

Ingredients

225 g / 8 oz / 1 ½ cups strawberries, hulled and sliced

½ tsp salt

175 g / 6 oz / ¾ cup low-fat vanilla custard

110 g / 4 oz / ½ cup low-fat Greek yogurt

125 g / 4 ½ oz piece of sponge cake, cut into chunks (sugar-free sponge cakes available in most supermarkets)

a few sprigs of mint, to garnish

Method

1. Toss together the strawberries and salt in a mixing bowl. Cover and leave for 10 minutes.

2. Whisk together the low-fat custard and Greek yogurt until light and frothy.

3. Line the base of four serving glasses with chunks of sponge, then top with the strawberries and any accumulated juices.

4. Spoon over the frothy custard mixture and garnish with sprigs of mint.

5. Serve immediately.

Iced Lemon Mousse

Serves: 4
Preparation time: 2 hours 15 minutes
Cooking time: 5 minutes

Ingredients

2 tsp powdered gelatin

75 ml / 3 fl. oz / ⅓ cup sugar-free
  lemon squash

3 medium egg whites

½ tsp cream of tartar

a pinch of salt

1 lemon, zested

Method

1. Soften the gelatin in 2 tbsp of cold water in a bowl.
   Leave to stand for 5 minutes, then whisk.

2. Combine the squash with 250 ml / 9 fl. oz /
   1 cup of cold water in a saucepan. Warm over a
   medium heat, then whisk in the gelatin mixture.

3. Continue to cook for 2 minutes until the gelatin has
   dissolved. Set to one side to cool.

4. Meanwhile, beat the egg whites with a pinch of salt
   until soft peaks form. Add the cream of tartar and
   2 tbsp of the lemon cordial liquid and beat until
   stiffly peaked.

5. Divide the remaining lemon squash liquid between
   four serving glasses.

6. Top with the egg whites and freeze immediately for at
   least 2 hours.

7. Remove from the freezer and garnish with lemon zest
   before serving.

Pumpkin and Almond Cake

Serves: 8
Preparation time: 10 minutes
Cooking time: 50–60 minutes

Ingredients

300 g / 10 ½ oz / 2 cups canned pumpkin chunks, drained

1 tsp vanilla extract

½ tsp ground nutmeg

150 g / 5 oz / ²/₃ cups pumpkin purée, sweetened with agave or honey

3 medium eggs

150 ml / 5 fl. oz / ²/₃ cup sunflower oil

2 tbsp semi-skimmed milk

200 g / 7 oz / 1 ¹/₃ cups self-raising flour

55 g / 2 oz / ¹/₃ cup cornflour (cornstarch)

½ tsp baking powder

a pinch of salt

55 g / 2 oz / ½ cup ground almonds

2 tbsp flaked (slivered) almonds

Method

1. Preheat the oven to 160°C (140°C fan) / 325F / gas 3. Grease and line a 2 lb loaf tin.

2. Add 200 g of pumpkin, the nutmeg and vanilla extract to a food processor. Blitz until smooth.

3. Whisk together the pumpkin purée, eggs, oil and milk in a mixing jug until smooth.

4. Sift the flour, cornflour, baking powder and salt into a mixing bowl, then stir through the ground almonds and remaining pumpkin.

5. Add the wet ingredients to the dry and mix until just incorporated, then scrape into the prepared tin. Tap the tin a few times to release any trapped air bubbles, and scatter the flaked almonds on top.

6. Bake for 50–60 minutes until golden and risen; a toothpick should come out clean from the centre.

7. Remove to a wire rack to cool completely before turning out and slicing.

Light Raspberry Mousse

Serves: 4
Preparation time: 2 hours 10 minutes
Cooking time: 5 minutes

Ingredients

350 g / 12 oz / 2 ⅓ cups raspberries
½ lemon, juiced
400 g / 14 oz / 2 cups coconut cream, chilled
a pinch of cocoa powder, to garnish

Method

1. Combine 275 g of the raspberries with the lemon juice in a saucepan.

2. Cook over a medium heat, stirring occasionally, until the raspberries are soft and juicy; 4–5 minutes.

3. Purée the mixture in a food processor. Pass through a sieve into a small bowl and set to one side.

4. Whip the coconut cream in a mixing bowl with an electric mixer for 3–4 minutes until softly peaked.

5. Fold through the raspberry purée until evenly incorporated, then spoon into glasses. Cover and chill for 2 hours.

6. Serve the mousses with the reserved raspberries on top and a pinch of cocoa powder as a garnish.

Fromage Blanc and Bilberry Pie

Serves: 8
Preparation time: 15–20 minutes
Cooking time: 20–25 minutes

Ingredients

250 g / 9 oz ready-made lighter shortcrust pastry

a little plain (all-purpose) flour, for dusting

1 small egg, beaten

350 g / 12 oz / 1 ½ cups fromage blanc

350 g / 12 oz / 1 ½ cups vanilla yogurt

1 tbsp lemon juice

½ tsp vanilla extract

300 g / 10 ½ oz / 2 cups bilberries (use blueberries if not available)

Method

1. Preheat the oven to 180°C (160°C fan) / 350F / gas 4. Roll out the pastry on a floured surface into a round roughly ½ cm (¼ in) thick. Use to line the base and sides of a 20 cm (8 in) fluted tart tin. Trim any excess pastry and discard, then prick the base all over with a fork.

2. Line with greaseproof paper and fill with baking beans, then blind bake for 15 minutes. Remove from the oven and discard the greaseproof paper and baking beans.

3. Return the pastry to the oven for 5 minutes to brown the base. Brush with the beaten egg, then return to the oven for another 2 minutes.

4. Allow to cool. Beat together the fromage blanc, yogurt, lemon juice and vanilla extract.

5. Remove the pastry from the tin, then fill with the fromage blanc filling. Top with most of the bilberries, serving the rest on the side as a garnish.

Buckwheat Waffles

Serves: 4
Preparation time: 10 minutes
Cooking time: 15 minutes

Ingredients

150 g / 5 oz / 1 cup plain (all-purpose) flour

150 g / 5 oz / 1 cup buckwheat flour

1 tbsp baking powder

½ tsp salt

2 large eggs, beaten

375 ml / 13 fl. oz / 1 ½ cups
    semi-skimmed milk

75 g / 3 oz / ⅓ cup unsalted butter, melted

½ tsp vanilla extract

1 tbsp sunflower oil

300 g / 10 ½ oz / 2 cups strawberries,
    hulled and halved

100 g / 3 ½ oz / ⅔ cup soft goats'
    cheese, cubed

a small handful of sorrel leaves

freshly ground black pepper

Method

1. Sift together the flours, baking powder and salt into a large mixing bowl.

2. Beat together the eggs, milk, melted butter and vanilla extract in a mixing jug. Slowly add to the dry ingredients, whisking at the same time until you have a smooth batter.

3. Preheat a waffle iron to hot and wipe the surface with sunflower oil. Ladle the batter into the iron and close. Cook according to manufacturer's instructions until the waffles are golden. Repeat this method to cook the batter until you have four large waffles.

4. Roughly mash half of the strawberries and set to one side. Stack the waffles in bowls and top with mashed strawberries, halved strawberries and some goats' cheese.

5. Garnish with sorrel leaves and a little black pepper before serving.

Carob Coconut Vegan Cake

Makes: 16 squares
Preparation time: 15 minutes
Cooking time: 40–45 minutes

Ingredients

250 g / 9 oz / 1 $^2/_3$ cups carob chips

150 g / 5 oz / ¾ cup silken tofu

250 ml / 9 fl. oz / 1 cup coconut milk

175 ml / 6 fl. oz / ¾ cup sunflower oil

110 g / 4 oz / $^2/_3$ cup cocoa powder, sifted

400 g / 14 oz / 2 $^2/_3$ cups self-raising flour, sifted

1 tsp bicarbonate of (baking) soda

2 tbsp desiccated coconut

2 tbsp flaked (slivered) almonds, toasted

Method

1. Preheat the oven to 180°C (160°C fan) / 350F / gas 4. Grease and line a 20 cm (8 in)square cake tin with greaseproof paper.

2. Melt the carob chips in a bain-marie set over a pan of simmering water. Stir until melted, then set to one side to cool.

3. Combine the tofu, coconut milk, sunflower oil, cocoa powder, flour and bicarbonate of soda in a food processor. Blitz until smooth, then pour into a mixing bowl.

4. Fold through the melted carob chips until incorporated, then scrape the batter into the cake tin and bake for 40–45 minutes.

5. Remove to a wire rack to cool completely, then turn out and cut into squares. Garnish with desiccated coconut and flaked almonds.

Chocolate and Raspberry Mousse

Serves: 4
Preparation time: 1 hour 10 minutes
Cooking time: 5 minutes

Ingredients

350 g / 12 oz / 2 ⅓ cups raspberries
½ lemon, juiced
400 g / 14 oz / 2 cups coconut cream, chilled
2 tbsp cocoa powder
1 tsp vanilla extract
½ tsp xanthan gum

Method

1. Combine three-quarters of the raspberries with the lemon juice in a saucepan set over a medium heat; cook until softened and juicy.

2. Purée the mixture in a food processor and pass through a sieve into a bowl.

3. Scrape the coconut cream into a bowl and add the cocoa powder, vanilla extract and xanthan gum; beat with an electric mixer for 4–5 minutes until thick and softly peaked.

4. Spoon the raspberry purée into the base of four small serving glasses before topping with the remaining raspberries.

5. Spoon the chocolate mousse on top; cover and chill for 1 hour before serving.

Chocolate Flapjack Bites

Makes: 35
Preparation time: 30 minutes
Cooking time: 30 minutes

Ingredients

2 ripe bananas

100 ml / 3 ½ fl. oz / ⅓ cup raw honey

100 g / 3 ½ oz / ½ cup butter

450 g / 1 lb / 4 ½ cups rolled porridge oats

200 g / 7 oz / 1 ⅓ cups sugar-free milk
  chocolate

Method

1. Preheat the oven to 190°C (170°C fan) / 375F / gas 5 and grease and line a 20 cm x 28 cm (8 in x 11 in) tray bake tin with greaseproof paper.

2. Put the bananas in a blender with the honey and butter and blend until smooth. Stir in the oats then spoon into a greased baking tin and level the surface.

3. Bake for 30 minutes or until golden brown and cooked through.

4. Cut into 4 cm (1 ½ in) squares while still warm, but leave to cool completely before removing from the tin.

5. Melt the chocolate in a microwave or bain-marie, then dip each flapjack and leave to set on a sheet of greaseproof paper.

Strawberry Tart

Serves: 8
Preparation time: 1 hour 40 minutes
Cooking time: 25 minutes

Ingredients

110 g / 4 oz / ½ cup butter, cubed and chilled

225 g / 8 oz / 1 ½ cups plain (all-purpose) flour

500 ml / 17 ½ fl. oz / 2 cups milk

1 vanilla pod, halved lengthways

100 ml / 3 ½ fl. oz / ½ cup raw honey

4 large egg yolks

2 tbsp cornflour (cornstarch)

250 g / 9 oz / 1 ⅔ cups strawberries, halved

12 g sachet powdered gelatin

1 tbsp lemon juice

mint leaves to garnish

Method

1. Preheat the oven to 200°C (180°C fan) / 400F / gas 6.

2. Rub the butter into the flour then stir in just enough cold water to make a pliable dough.

3. Roll out the pastry and use it to line a 23 cm (9 in) round tart tin. Line it with cling film and baking beans and bake for 10 minutes. Remove the film and beans and bake for 5 minutes.

4. Heat the milk and vanilla pod until it starts to simmer, then leave to infuse for 5 minutes. Stir 85 ml of honey into the egg yolks and cornflour, then gradually whisk in the milk, discarding the vanilla pod. Transfer it to the saucepan and stir over a medium heat until it thickens. Spoon it into the tart case and leave to cool. Arrange the strawberries on top.

5. Sprinkle the gelatin into 100 ml of hot water and wait for 1 minute. Stir until dissolved then add the lemon juice and the final tablespoon of honey. Chill for 15 minutes or until it starts to gel, then spoon it over the tart. Serve garnished with mint leaves.

Treats and Snacks

Treats and Snacks

Snacking can be one of the biggest pitfalls for someone going sugar-free. If your body is used to the constant highs and lows of a sugar-heavy diet, you will probably crave frequent snacks between meals. Unfortunately, some of the most convenient snacks are loaded with sugar.

As you change your diet to a slow-burning, nutrient-rich plan, you will feel fuller for longer and have fewer cravings. But there's no harm in keeping your energy up throughout the day with a healthy snack here and there.

There are loads of options for healthy snacks. A handful of nuts, for example, is packed with protein, so why not keep some handy in your bag or your desk drawer? Vegetables dipped in hummus make another great choice. There are so many delicious options available that once you have ditched the biscuits, you will never look back!

Guacamole Tartlets

- -

Makes: 12
Preparation time: 10 minutes
Cooking time: 5 minutes

- -

Ingredients

2 large ripe avocados, halved and pitted

2 cloves of garlic, minced

2 limes, juiced

1 tsp hot sauce

a small bunch of coriander (cilantro), chopped

12 small savoury tart shells

2 button mushrooms, sliced

1 stick of celery, peeled and thinly sliced

½ tsp Cayenne pepper

salt and freshly ground black pepper

Method

1. Roughly chop the avocado flesh and add to a food processor along with the garlic, lime juice, hot sauce, most of the coriander and some seasoning.

2. Blitz the mixture until smooth, and adjust the seasoning to taste.

3. Spoon the smooth guacamole into the tart shells and arrange on serving plates.

4. Top with sliced mushroom and celery as well as a pinch of cayenne and the remaining coriander as a garnish.

5. Serve immediately for best results.

Sweet Potato Crisps

Serves: 4
Preparation time: 15–20 minutes
Cooking time: 18–20 minutes

Ingredients

2 medium sweet potatoes, peeled

2 tbsp sunflower oil

½ tsp paprika

1 tsp salt

2 tbsp desiccated coconut, to serve

Method

1. Preheat the oven to 160°C (140°C fan) / 325F / gas 3.

2. Thinly slice the sweet potatoes into very thin slices using a mandolin. Collect the slices in a large mixing bowl.

3. Pat the slices dry, then toss with the sunflower oil, paprika and salt.

4. Arrange the slices on two large baking trays, making sure they are in a single layer.

5. Bake for 18–22 minutes until the edges start to curl and the tops are dry.

6. Remove the trays to a wire racks to cool.

7. Once cool, serve with desiccated coconut on the side.

Roquefort and Walnut Crostini

Makes: 16
Preparation time: 10 minutes
Cooking time: 5 minutes

Ingredients

4 slices of white sandwich bread

110 g / 4 oz piece of Roquefort

16 walnut halves

2 tbsp runny honey (optional)

Method

1. Toast the slices of bread in a toaster or under a hot grill until golden brown.

2. Remove from the grill and cut into quarters.

3. Cut the piece of Roquefort into small bite-sized chunks. Arrange on the toasts along with a walnut half.

4. Drizzle with honey (if using) before serving.

Mozzarella Balls

Serves: 8 (as an appetiser)
Preparation time: 10 minutes
Cooking time: 5 minutes

Ingredients

8 slices of prosciutto

16 small fresh mozzarella balls, drained

110 ml / 4 fl. oz / ½ cup extra-virgin olive oil

75 g / 3 oz / ¾ cup shelled pistachios, crushed

16 wooden toothpicks

a small handful of basil leaves

salt and freshly ground black pepper

Method

1. Cut the slices of prosciutto in half. Dip the balls of mozzarella into the olive oil and then coat in the crushed pistachios.

2. Wrap in pieces of prosciutto and secure with a toothpick.

3. Cover and chill until ready to serve. Garnish with some basil leaves and a little salt and pepper.

Gluten-free Raisin Brioche

Serves: 8
Preparation time: 1 ¾–2 ¼ hours
Cooking time: 20–25 minutes

Ingredients

250 g / 9 oz / 1 ²/₃ cups gluten-free plain (all-purpose) flour

110 g / 4 oz / ½ cup unsalted butter, cold and cubed

1 ½ tbsp fast-action dried yeast

a pinch of salt

3 medium eggs

150 g / 5 oz / 1 cup raisins

1 medium egg yolk, beaten

Method

1. Combine the flour and butter in a food process and pulse until it resembles fine breadcrumbs. Stir in the yeast and salt, then tip into a bowl.

2. Add the eggs and mix until a soft dough forms. Continue to knead for 4–5 minutes, then add the raisins and knead for a further minute.

3. Divide the dough into 8 and shape into balls, then drop into individual, lined moulds or ramekins. Cover loosely with oiled cling film and leave to rise in a warm place for 1 ½–2 hours or until doubled in size.

4. Preheat the oven to 190°C (170°C fan) / 375F / gas 5. Place the moulds on a baking tray and brush the tops of the dough with beaten egg yolk.

5. Bake for 20–25 minutes until golden on top and risen. Remove to wire racks to cool before serving.

Oat, Linseed and Flax Bars

Serves: 8
Preparation time: 10 minutes
Cooking time: 15–20 minutes

Ingredients

300 g / 10 ½ oz / 2 cups rolled oats

2 tbsp flaxseeds

2 tbsp linseeds

150 g / 5 oz / ²⁄₃ cup apple sauce

55 g / 2 oz / ¼ cup reduced-fat margarine

a pinch of salt

Method

1. Preheat the oven to 180°C (160°C fan) / 350F / gas 4 and line a 18 cm (7 in) square baking tin with greaseproof paper.

2. Combine the oats, flaxseeds and linseeds in a large mixing bowl.

3. Melt together the apple sauce, margarine and salt in a pan set over a medium heat.

4. Whisk until smooth, then pour over the oats. Stir well to combine, then pack the mixture into the prepared tin.

5. Bake for 15–20 minutes until golden on top.

6. Remove the tin to a wire rack to cool completely, then turn out and cut into bars.

7. Serve immediately or store for up to three days in an airtight container.

Ice Cream Cookies

Makes: 16
Preparation time: 45 minutes, plus freezing time
Cooking time: 15 minutes

Ingredients

For the ice cream:

4 large eggs, separated

100 ml / 3 ½ oz / ½ cup raw honey

300 ml / 10 ½ fl. oz / 1 ¼ cups double (heavy) cream

For the cookies:

325 g / 11 ½ oz / 1 ¾ cups coconut sugar

175 g / 6 oz / 3/4 cup butter, melted

1 vanilla pod, seeds only

1 egg, plus 1 egg yolk

200 g / 7 oz / 1 ⅓ cups self-raising flour

50 g / 1/3 oz / ½ cup unsweetened cocoa powder

50 g / 1 ¾ oz / ½ cup pecan nuts, chopped

Method

1. Whisk the egg whites until they form stiff peaks and set aside. In a separate bowl, whisk the egg yolks with the honey until light and fluffy. In a third bowl, whip the cream until it holds its shape, then fold in the honey mixture, followed by the egg white.

2. Scrape the mixture into a freezer-proof container and freeze for 3 hours.

3. Preheat the oven to 160°C (140°C fan) / 325F / gas 3 and line two baking sheets with greaseproof paper.

4. Cream together the sugar, butter and vanilla seeds until pale and well whipped then beat in the egg and yolk, followed by the flour, cocoa and pecans.

5. Drop tablespoons of the mixture onto the prepared trays, leaving plenty of room to spread. Bake the cookies in batches for 15 minutes or until the edges are starting to crisp, but the centres are still chewy. Transfer to a wire rack and leave to cool completely.

6. To serve, sandwich the cookies together in pairs with a big scoop of ice cream.

Chocolate Rice Cakes

Makes: 8
Preparation time: 15 minutes
Cooking time: 5 minutes

Ingredients

150 g / 5 oz / 1 cup dark (90% cocoa) chocolate, chopped

8 plain rice cakes

2 tbsp desiccated coconut

Method

1. Place the chopped chocolate in a bain-marie set atop a saucepan of gently simmering water.

2. Stir occasionally until the chocolate has melted. Remove from the heat and leave to cool for 5 minutes.

3. Brush one side of the rice cakes with the melted chocolate using a pastry brush.

4. Sprinkle the tops of half with desiccated coconut. Leave the rice cakes to set on a wire rack before serving.

Puffed Rice Chocolate Bars

Serves: 8
Preparation time: 2 hours 15 minutes
Cooking time: 5 minutes

Ingredients

125 g / 4 ½ oz / 5 cups puffed rice

100 g / 3 ½ oz / ²/₃ cup rolled oats

225 g / 8 oz / 1 ½ cups dark (90% cocoa) chocolate, chopped

55 g / 2 oz / ¹/₃ cup cocoa powder

55 ml / 2 fl. oz / ¼ cup semi-skimmed milk

Method

1. Grease and line an 20 cm (8 in) square baking tin with greaseproof paper.

2. Combine the puffed rice and oats in a large mixing bowl, then stir and set to one side.

3. Melt the chocolate in a bain-marie set atop a saucepan of simmering water.

4. Stir occasionally until the chocolate has melted. Remove from the heat and leave to cool slightly, then add to the rice and oats. Stir, then add the cocoa powder and milk.

5. Stir thoroughly until combined, then pack the mixture into the prepared baking tin.

6. Cover and chill for 2 hours until set.

7. Turn out the bar and cut into slices before serving.

No-sugar Financiers

Makes: approximately 18
Preparation time: 15 minutes
Cooking time: 6–8 minutes

Ingredients

125 g / 4 ½ oz / 1 ¼ cups ground almonds

3 small very ripe bananas, mashed

100 g / 3 ½ oz / ⅔ cup self-raising flour

a pinch of salt

150 g / 5 oz / ⅔ cup reduced-fat margarine, melted

4 large egg whites

powdered stevia for dusting

Method

1. Preheat the oven to 230°C (210°C fan) / 450F / gas 8 and grease two 12-hole financier moulds.

2. Combine the ground almonds, banana, flour and salt in a food processor. Blitz until smooth.

3. Add the egg whites and pulse until incorporated. Add the melted margarine and pulse again until a pourable batter forms.

4. Spoon the batter into the moulds and bake for 6–8 minutes until golden and risen.

5. Remove to a wire rack to cool completely before turning out and serving.

6. Dust with powdered stevia.

Flapjacks

Serves: 8
Preparation time: 15 minutes
Cooking time: 20–25 minutes

Ingredients

55 g / 2 oz / ¼ cup reduced-fat margarine

1 small banana, mashed

100 g / 3 ½ oz / ½ cup apple sauce

300 g / 10 ½ oz / 2 cups rolled oats

300 g / 10 ½ oz / 1 ½ cups low-fat cream cheese, softened

1 tsp vanilla extract

Method

1. Preheat the oven to 180°C (160°C fan) / 350F / gas 4. Grease and line an 18 cm (7 in) square baking tin with greaseproof paper.

2. Melt the butter in a saucepan set over a moderate heat. Pour into a food processor and blitz with the banana and apple sauce.

3. Scrape into a mixing bowl and add the oats. Mix thoroughly until combined.

4. Pack the mixture into the prepared tin, levelling the top with the back of a tablespoon. Bake for 20–25 minutes until golden on top before removing to a wire rack.

Popcorn Nut Bars

Serves: 18
Preparation time: 40 minutes
Cooking time: 5 minutes

Ingredients

125 g / 4 ½ oz / 12 cups plain popcorn
(popped)

150 g / 5 oz / 1 cup rolled oats

75 g / 3 oz / ¾ cup walnuts, chopped

100 g / 3 ½ oz / ⅔ cup raisins

2 tbsp almonds, chopped

2 tbsp Brazil nuts, chopped

¾ tsp ground cinnamon

175 g / 6 oz / ¾ cup reduced-fat margarine

Method

1. Grease and line the base and sides of two rectangular 32 cm x 18 cm (13 in x 7 in) cake tins with greaseproof paper.

2. Combine the popped popcorn, rolled oats, walnuts, raisins, almonds, Brazil nuts and ground cinnamon in a large mixing bowl.

3. Melt the margarine in a saucepan set over a low heat. Once melted, leave to cool slightly and pour over the popcorn.

4. Mix well to coat thoroughly, then pack the mixture into the prepared tins. Make sure that the tops are flat and even using the back of a tablespoon.

5. Chill for at least 30 minutes before turning out, slicing, and serving.

Pure Juice Ice Lollies

Makes: 2 of each flavour
Preparation time: 15 minutes
Freezing time: 4 hours

Ingredients

Red lollies:

2 beetroot, quartered

2 red apples, quartered

150 g / 5 ½ oz / 1 cup raspberries

Yellow lollies:

150 g / 5 ½ oz / 1 cup butternut squash, cubed

1 yellow pepper, quartered

2 mangoes, stoned and cut into chunks

Green lollies:

3 kiwi fruit, quartered

½ head broccoli, broken into florets

½ honeydew melon, peeled and cut into chunks

Method

1. For each type of lolly, process the ingredients through an electronic juicer, according to the manufacturer's instructions.

2. Divide each type of juice between two holes of a 6-hole ice lolly maker.

3. Freeze for 4 hours or until solid before unmoulding and serving.

Meal Plans and Diary

Meal Plans and Diary

When starting a new diet, it is important to have a plan. Otherwise you will have a day – probably fairly early on – where you are pressed for time and don't have a menu planned or ingredients bought. It is at times like this when you are likely to reach for something comforting and familiar…and possibly full of sugar.

Before you start, sit down and think about how you want to tackle going sugar-free. How far do you want to reduce your sugar intake each week? You should have a plan for how many grams of sugar you are allowed as you gradually cut it out of your diet. Also, jot down some targets for exercise and weight loss. It may seem like a lot to think about, but once you get into the swing of things, it will all become second nature.

In this chapter, you can plan and track your progress for ten weeks. The ideas and recipes in this book are only the tip of the iceberg as far as delicious sugar-free food is concerned!

Once you have your plan in place and your shopping list written, make sure to keep a record of everything you eat and drink. That way you cannot just 'forget' about that biscuit with your tea or soft drink or glass of wine at a friend's. Before you know it, you will be sugar-free!

Week 1

	Breakfast	Lunch	Snack	Dinner
Monday				
Tuesday				
Wednesday				
Thursday				
Friday				
Saturday				
Sunday				

Starting weight

Finishing weight

How I feel	Exercise log

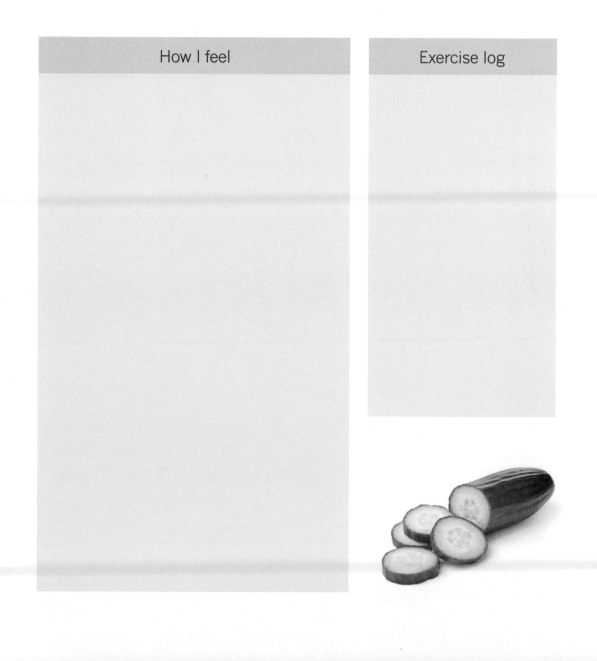

Week 2

	Breakfast	Lunch	Snack	Dinner
Monday				
Tuesday				
Wednesday				
Thursday				
Friday				
Saturday				
Sunday				

Starting weight

Finishing weight

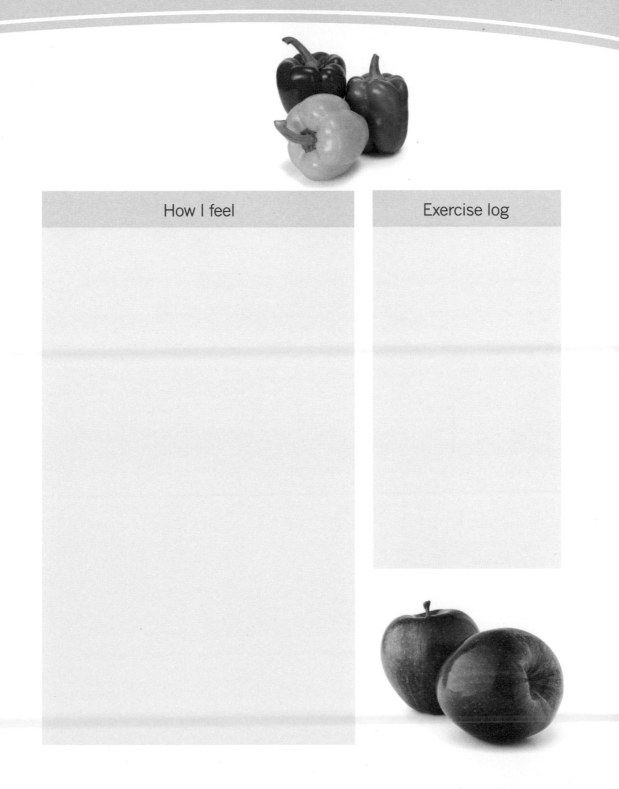

How I feel	Exercise log

Week 3

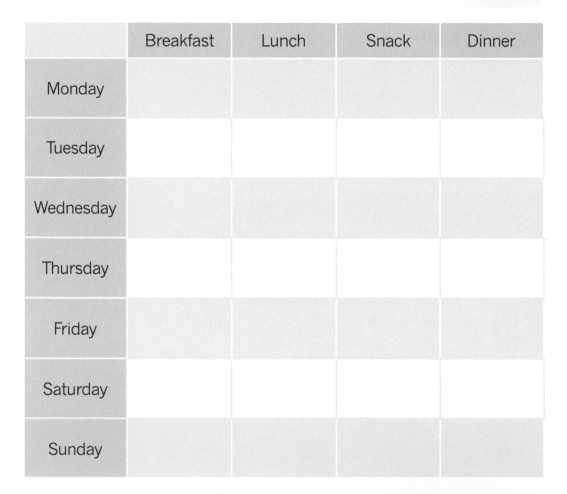

	Breakfast	Lunch	Snack	Dinner
Monday				
Tuesday				
Wednesday				
Thursday				
Friday				
Saturday				
Sunday				

Starting weight

Finishing weight

How I feel	Exercise log

Week 4

	Breakfast	Lunch	Snack	Dinner
Monday				
Tuesday				
Wednesday				
Thursday				
Friday				
Saturday				
Sunday				

Starting weight

Finishing weight

How I feel	Exercise log

Week 5

	Breakfast	Lunch	Snack	Dinner
Monday				
Tuesday				
Wednesday				
Thursday				
Friday				
Saturday				
Sunday				

Starting weight

Finishing weight

How I feel

Exercise log

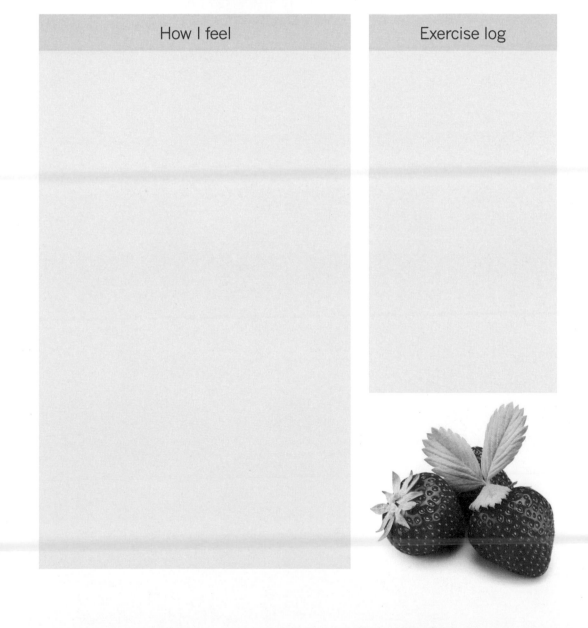

Week 6

	Breakfast	Lunch	Snack	Dinner
Monday				
Tuesday				
Wednesday				
Thursday				
Friday				
Saturday				
Sunday				

Starting weight

Finishing weight

How I feel	Exercise log

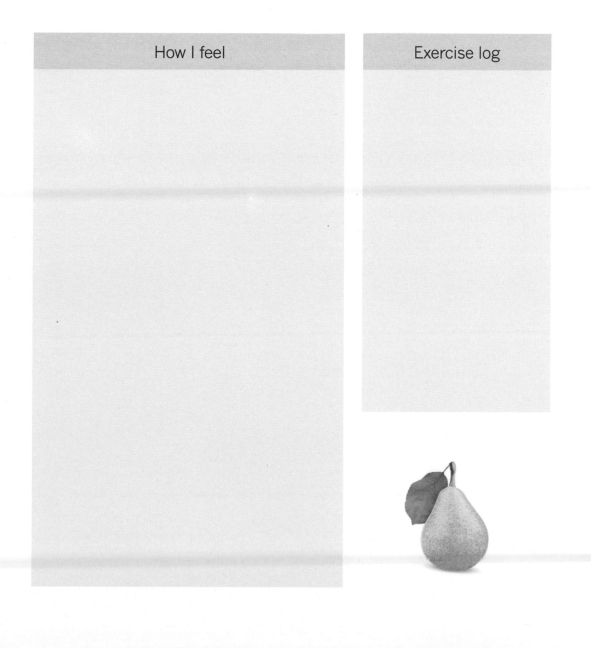

Week 7

	Breakfast	Lunch	Snack	Dinner
Monday				
Tuesday				
Wednesday				
Thursday				
Friday				
Saturday				
Sunday				

Starting weight

Finishing weight

How I feel	Exercise log

Week 8

	Breakfast	Lunch	Snack	Dinner
Monday				
Tuesday				
Wednesday				
Thursday				
Friday				
Saturday				
Sunday				

Starting weight

Finishing weight

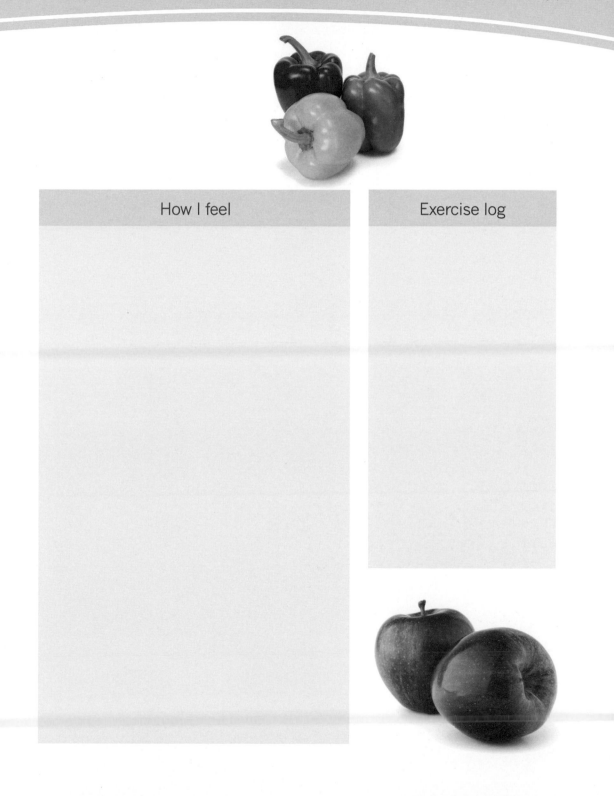

How I feel	Exercise log

Week 9

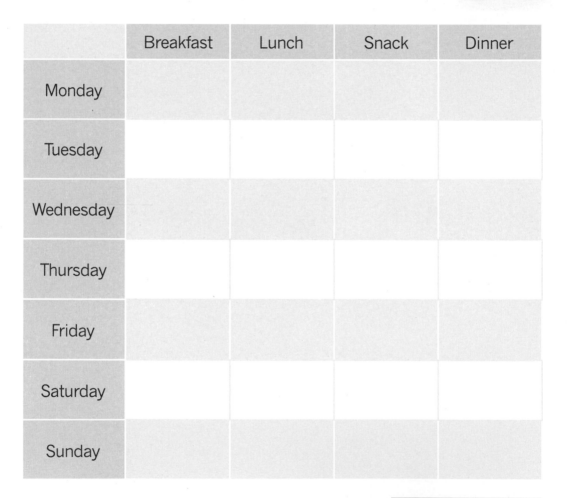

	Breakfast	Lunch	Snack	Dinner
Monday				
Tuesday				
Wednesday				
Thursday				
Friday				
Saturday				
Sunday				

Starting weight

Finishing weight

How I feel	Exercise log

Week 10

	Breakfast	Lunch	Snack	Dinner
Monday				
Tuesday				
Wednesday				
Thursday				
Friday				
Saturday				
Sunday				

Starting weight

Finishing weight

How I feel	Exercise log

Keeping It Off

Congratulations – you've done it! You've stuck to the sugar-free diet and are feeling the benefits already. You have more energy, you feel great, and you have lost some weight. Now comes the hard part: keeping it off. Many dieters reach their target and then lose the momentum to stick with the new routine. Here are a few tips for keeping motivated:

- Remember why you did it! Have a look at an old photograph of yourself and think about how you felt before you cut out sugar. Keep that old photo handy for whenever you have a craving or are feeling low

- If you have gone down a dress size, then clear out some of your old clothes, and treat yourself to a few things in your new size

- Set a new target. For example, now that you are healthier and fitter, maybe you could train for a fun run or even a half marathon. Keeping focused on goals can help keep you from backtracking

- Keep track. Weigh yourself once a week and give yourself a pat on the back every time you maintain your target weight
- Set an example. Your friends and family will notice how much better you are looking and feeling. Helping someone else to cut out sugar can keep you motivated to stick with it yourself

If you have cut out sugar entirely and are still craving a few favourite sweet treats even after months of sticking to your diet, then there is no harm in reintroducing it in small amounts. As long as you stay well within the recommended guidelines, an occasional small treat will not hurt. If you have stuck to the sugar-free diet then you know you have the willpower to keep your sugar intake under control. Moderation is the key!

Notes

Notes

Notes

Notes

Notes

Notes

Diet consultant: Jo Stimpson.

Main food photography and recipe development: © StockFood UK.

All other recipe images courtesy of Thinkstock, Getty Images, iStock.

Cover: main idildemir/iStock; other © StockFood UK.

Flap: © StockFood UK.

Picture Credits
4 Dmitri Mihhailov/Shutterstock; 6 Matej Kastelic/ Shutterstock; 7 saurabhpbhoyar/Shutterstock; 8 picsfive/Shutterstock; 10 markos86/Shutterstock; 12t Elena Schweitzer/Dreamstime; 12b Jocic / Dreamstime; 14 Richard Thomas/Dreamstime; 16 Africa Studio/Shutterstock; 21 Peter Bernik/ Shutterstock; 22 B. and E. Dudzinscy/Shutterstock; 24 Steigele /Dreamstime; 25 Georgii Dolgykh/ Dreamstime; 26 Monkey Business Images/ Dreamstime; 28 Stephen Mcsweeny/Shutterstock; 31 Alejandro Salvador Mir/iStock; 32 Kladej/ Shutterstock; 34 Legaa/Dreamstime; 37 Ildipapp/ Dreamstime; 38 Paul Maguire/Dreamstime; 39 Goran Bogicevic/Dreamstime; 41 Monkey Business Images /Shutterock; 43 Darren Baker/Dreamstime; 46 Andrey Arkusha/Shutterstock; 47 Aleksi/ Shutterstock; 47 Diana Valujeva /Dreamstime; 49 tmcphotos/Dreamstime; 50 Gavran333/Shutterstock; 52 Golyak/Dreamstime; 53 Yellowj/Shutterstock; 223 Photographerlondon/Dreamstime; 225 B. and E. Dudzinscy/Shutterstock; 226 jf123/Dreamstime; 227 Anna Sedneva/Shutterstock; 228 Marazen/ Dreamstime; 229 Mariusz Blach/Dreamstime; 230 Mohaned Osama/Dreamstime; 231 Dionisvera / Shutterstock; 232 Alexander Pladdet/Dreamstime; 233 Alexstar/Dreamstime; 234 Maks Narodenko/ Shutterstock; 235 Elovich/Shutterstock; 236 Duskbabe/Dreamstime; 237 Roman Samokhin/ Dreamstime; 246 aaron belford/Shutterstock; 248 Ariwasabi/Dreamstime; 256 Warren Goldswain/Shutterstock; 238 jf123/Dreamstime; 239 Anna Sedneva/Shutterstock; 240 Marazen/ Dreamstime; 241 Mariusz Blach/Dreamstime; 242 Mohaned Osama/Dreamstime; 243 Dionisvera / Shutterstock; 244 Alexander Pladdet/Dreamstime; 245 Alexstar/Dreamstime; iStock: 9, 11, 13, 15, 17, 18, 23, 27, 29, 30, 33, 35, 36, 40, 42, 44, 45, 51, 54/5, 58t, 62t, 66t, 69t, 70t, 73t, 74t, 77t, 81t, 82t, 85t, 86/7, 94t, 97, 98t, 101t, 105t, 106t, 109t, 110t, 114t, 116, 117t, 119, 121, 124, 136t, 139t, 139b, 143t, 144t, 155t, 157, 158/9, 174, 181, 187, 188, 190/1, 198t, 201t, 202, 220/1, 222, 224, 247, 249, 251, 253, 255.